MADE FOR RELATIONSHIP

Dr Abimbola Adewumi Alabi

Drink water from your own cistern,
running water from your own well.

Proverbs 5:15

XULON PRESS

Xulon Press
2301 Lucien Way #415
Maitland, FL 32751
407.339.4217
www.xulonpress.com

Unless otherwise indicated, Scripture quotations taken from the King James Version (KJV)—*public domain.*

Printed in the United States of America.

ISBN-13: 9781545606209

Table of Contents

ACKNOWLEDGMENTS

I acknowledge Elshaddai my maker who sent me into this world and gave me the opportunity to His empowering people to fulfill their God-given assignment in life.

I also acknowledge, with enormous gratitude, beloved friends, colleagues, and mentors, whom God sent into my life at various seasons and for various reasons.

Special editorial thanks go Sister Modupe Ogunbiyi, Yemi Folorunsho, Anthony Oluyinka Adesile, Onyeoma Molokwu, Jonathan Olakunle and Amelia Harper.

If I have seen further, it is only by standing on the shoulders of giants. I thank my wife and friend Olutoyin for making this book a reality, and continuously adding value to my life. Thanks to my uncles from Ikirun, Toke Iyanda (Late), Layi Afolabi and E Olaninyi, who were there early, saw, and nurtured the potential in me.

Thanks to Prof. Esther Aderibigbe for being used of the Lord to draw me to the TRUTH. Thanks to Bishop Francis Wale Oke, Dr. Samuel Olusegun Odunaike, Dr Wilson Badejo and Dr.Gabriel Olusoji Farombi, for the structural foundation of knowing and serving HIM. Thanks to Prof Nurudeen Alao who taught me to study very hard and to keep studying. Thanks to Bunmi Oni, Dr Chris Imoisili, and my father-in-law, Oba Onafuwa. I am also grateful for my Forever Friends Lanre Amos (late), Abiodun Fijabi, Tunde Ojo, Kehinde Lawanson and Greg Okubo.

Finally, a big thank you to my sons Tolu & Temi for being such wonderful friends. I also want to express appreciation to our members of great families.

Abimbola Adewumi Alabi

The events in this book are true and are based on my life and the testimony of others. Some names and locations were changed to protect their privacy.

DEDICATION

In this one life, God gave me a privilege to find and choose a true relationship in my friend, lover, prayer partner and wife - Olutoyin.

I dedicate this book to Olutoyin Adebusola Alabi (Nee Onafuwa):

Sharing this life with you is the only purposeful relationship for me.

FOREWORD

'Relationship' is one word that describes the underlying theme of this book. When we choose whom to interact with, the depth of such interaction grows out of knowledge and trust in the relationship. The capacity to cultivate, grow and maintain long term relationships is, in turn, determined by our relationship with God. As the hub connects the bicycle wheel to the power source through the spokes so that the drive from the pedals results in positive motion, our relationships also survive if the center holds like the hub when we have a live connection to the transforming power of God through the new birth in Christ. This primary vertical relationship to God impacts the horizontal relationships we have with others beyond the imagination of the human mind with. Yet this is what gives us meaning.

Much of our adolescent life we search for significance, and this sometimes takes us through wild and riotous terrain until God's mercy catches up with us, opening our eyes to the one ally we always ignored. The abundance of social media platforms, information and infinite choices we have to make, further complicates matters even further and subconsciously choreographs our daily routine in ways we never imagined. As the world gets smaller and every other person is now only six degrees away, information is democratized in a way that it never was before. This unlimited open access also comes with the burden of freedom: the responsibility for making choices that help secure our vertical and horizontal relationships.

Now and again someone wants to share their experience of the search for meaning in the world, and this book reveals one such experience. In its pages, we gain a glimpse into the chronicles of a young man's emergence from the modest environment of a superstitious up country life and his tutoring by a God-fearing father who lived for the liberation of his offspring from the pangs of illiteracy. Associated poverty by first putting himself through the rigors of adult education. We follow his struggles through bachelorhood, the challenge of building enduring relationships, and the changes that he experienced once he saw the Light and found his soul mate.

Life is made up of, sometimes overlapping series of experiences: we live it forward but learn it backward. Experience nevertheless remains the best teacher, but a very hard grader. She gives you the test first and the lesson later – and we have to come to terms with this order of things as we live from day to day. She is not totally unkind, however, because she dispenses the doses of experiences in measures that we can assimilate if we pay close attention; and the sequence of such experiences often is such that the lesson at each post is a pre-requisite for, and a guide through, the next test. Our success through life is therefore measured by how well we internalize the lessons that have been placed as milestones along the journey.

Our natural instinct is to wish the tough tests away or wonder why we deserve such testing, but these tests are meant to be stepping stones, not obstacles. A man is not defined by any experience or event, however terrible or heart-warming, but by how he responds to the experiences and learns the lessons. God allows experiences and events to teach us to depend on Him. We tend to understand this more from unpleasant experiences – loss of job, betrayal by a trusted friend, loss of a loved one or divorce. However, the great experiences of life which make us glad and which we crave, are meant to do no less. Whatever we face, our source of joy should not be dependent on the experiences we go through, but on our enduring relationship with our Maker. We will only appreciate the peaks because of the valleys; and when life deals sour lemons, it is an invitation to make lemonade.

The Savior modeled that for us in the way He spent the short period of His incarnation on the earth. He guarded His relationship with His Father, because it is the only one that would see Him through the dark patches of being the sacrificial Lamb. To maintain this critical relationship, He got up at the crack of dawn, often going into secluded places to commune with the Father without interference. As a result, He did not revile His betrayer, and, instead, prayed for the people who pierced Him and hung Him on the Cross. He allowed nothing that could endanger the fellowship from this relationship. He experienced our emotions too, for He once felt depressed to the point of weeping. He is able to guide us through life because He has been in our skin and experienced the frailties and limitations of humanity. We therefore find fulfillment when we find the Savior and are enabled to respond to life issues the way He did.

-Bunmi Oni

INTRODUCTION

"I know the way you are now. I bet I can correctly predict your next move. I could write a book about you,"

Diana's words echoed in my head as I made my way back to my room from the telephone on the hallway wall.

Lying on my bed, I pondered her words. How could Diana who had not seen me in three years, and was in far-away tin-mining city of Jos, over eight hundred kilometers away from me in Lagos, Nigeria's mega metropolis, actually predict what I could or could not do? Was I so transparent, she could so easily read me?

Diana and I met at the writers' family Club of the Lagos Varsity Christian Union (LVCU), and through the activities of the Club , worked together to fulfill our desire to proclaim the Good News of Jesus Christ on the University campus. We did this through the publications Sunday Campus Preacher, and the Campus *Mirror* magazines.

Nigeria is not just the most populous country in Africa; every fifth African is Nigerian. Nigerians are mostly educated and, by destiny, can be found all over the world. Nigeria's size, economic potential and geographical location make it a pivotal nation. Indeed, someone once observed that if you imagine Africa as a hand gun pointing south, Nigeria is located where you might expect to find the trigger. A Federal Republic, Nigeria obtained independence from Britain on October 1, 1960 and has suffered misfortune in that the early indigenous leaders did not succeed in creating a truly home-grown democracy. It has been ruled, not governed or led, by both military and civilian governments. The country is endowed with some of the best and greatest natural and human resources in the world; but, over the years, it has had only self-seeking public office holders who never put the people first.

My conversation with Diana made me reflect back over many years. I thought about my growing up years, the futility of my life without Christ, and the deep confusions that had filled me. Finally, I thought about the hope Christ gave me when I received Him into my life, the many struggles and accomplishments of in my Christian race, the lessons I have learnt, and so on.

Looking back, turning page after page, I construed a bag full of life's truth that would counsel a new Christian and keep him/her on the kingdom track. that with God all things are possible and Mine is a reassuring story no matter the struggles and troubles he will face along the way the new Christian heeding the counsel will stand.

Penning my story also provided an opportunity for me to count my blessings full of God's grace and mercy. I couldn't have achieved anything if not for His grace. It is God's doing, and I am grateful for it.

I can remember where the thought sprang from, and it hit me faster than a tornado: I could write a book and recount through it, life's lessons He taught me through them, for the benefit of His fledgling Sheep.

Now, how about naming the book after my Lord, Jesus? *Made for Relationship* came to mind, and I believe it is a most appropriate title for this collection of my stories. all set and ready to go, this burning desire is what has put this book in your hands.

Made for Relationship is no ordinary storybook. It is a compilation of lessons learned from mistakes made and struggles overcome. It has also within it some eternal values to be cherished. We are living in the glorious age of the outpouring of the power of God. The gospel of grace, salvation, deliverance, blessing, and tremendous power is being preached more than ever before. This book calls us out of any euphoria of having made some impact and urges us further to break all fallow grounds, lay aside all weights and sins, and overcome the remaining hindrances that stand before us.

We have greater responsibilities as end-time saints to contend for the faith. Our precious faith is battling with some serious societal ills. We must shun frivolities and avoid deceptions, and do all we can to get the work at hand done. Our Darling Jesus will soon appear to rapture a holy, righteous, and blameless body.

Abimbola Adewumi Alabi

New York, USA

January 2012

Part One

Chapter 1

THE JOURNEY BEGINS

The twilight deepened. The sun had set, and the dim mist, and all it touched, colored silver and black. The goats and chickens that often ran freely through the village streets lay in their pens fast asleep. The cutlasses and hoes rested patiently for another day's work to begin. The market square was as quiet as a graveyard. The crickets chatted with one another in a language only they could understand. Nothing stirred. Another day's toil was over.

Somewhere in the quiet little town, young Matthew lay on his bed. His thoughts far beyond of Ikirun[1] pictures far above the familiar, quiet lives of the inhabitants of Ikirun. He envisioned himself in a higher institutions in the big city, learning the white man's ways and language. Indeed, what wouldn't he give to make that dream a reality? That picture would change the way things were in his Ikirun. He would impact many by teaching them everything learned. Illiteracy and poverty in Ikirun will be chased away by more glorious destinies.

Matthew would face a great many obstacles because, not many in Ikirun would share his grand picture. While he thought education would be the answer, most villagers loathed education as a time waster. If he had voiced his thoughts, he would have told him met a reprimand. The overarching occupation of the rustic inhabitants of the land was farming.

---

[1] An agricultural settlement in Osun State, Nigeria, known for its production of kola nuts.

What good would reading, 'riting, and 'rithmitic be to a farmer? How would teaching a child the three Rs of the white man benefit him?

"Besides, is it not all meant to make our children lazy dreamers," went the traditional thought. These were the villagers' beliefs, and they held on to them like a suckling child clings to his mother's breast.

Matthew knew he would get no support from home. His father had three wives and many children and his journey to literacy would have to be one he would embark upon by himself. He would have to take full responsibility for everything he needed to realise his picture. Matthew's resolve, therefore, could be likened to saying to the mountain Kilimanjaro I will surely get to your very top. Matthew somehow assuredly knew he could be what he wanted to be, and with his unexplainable but growing determination, he took the steps to make his dreams a reality.

While others went to farm business, Matthew enrolled in African Church[2] the Mission School of the many kilometers away from Ikirun. Every morning Matthew walked the distance alone. In no time, he graduated and gained admission into a higher institution of learning in the big city. Matthew's first wife could not understand his quest. Being traditional and uneducated, Matthew's first wife only believed all the big city quest was just a clever ploy by Matthew to marry someone else. As soon as Matthew left for the city, she split from Matthew and moved in with a rich farmer in a neighboring village, abandoning their three children with Matthew's mother.

Matthew's hard work, persistence, and commitment to his goals despite hindrances paid off. He became distinguished, not only amongst his father's children, but also in Ikirun. He was elevated to headmaster of the higher institution that was later established in the village and was popularly known as "Matthew the Teacher." He spent most of his time going from house to house, counseling parents and children alike of the benefits of education. His well known achievements made way for his mission to succeed with the people.

Seven years after Matthew's first wife abandoned ship, he met and married Felicia. Felicia, young and beautiful hailed from Offa was a graduating student at Matthew's school. She loved Matthew and made him happy from the day they got married. On June 30, 1960, a new baby Abimbola was born to the Matthew's family. She was a devoted mother to her children and stepchildren.

On the same day that I was born one of the great martyrs of Africa, Patrice Lumumba, was betrayed and killed in Belgian Congo. My father once narrated to me how some of his

---

2

A traditional African breakaway from the Anglican Communion, in Oshogbo, the capital city of Nigeria's Osun State

friends desired to name me after Lumumba, but he just did not agree with them at the time. How ironic, that years later, I knew by God that I should like Patrice Lumumba, lay my life down to help people fulfill their God-given destinies, as I strive to fulfill mine.

Revelation being progressive, I must admit that task has not come easy. As you will see, with each phase of my life, there have been moments that I moved far away and even have done things contradictory to that purpose. But God by His Word and great mercies continually made all things work together for good. Of course, leaving scars of my wrong choices and decisions. Just like the children of Israel's journey of 40 days turned into 40 years, so also, some attainments in my life were delayed as a consequence of my choices. However, we all ride on God's all-sufficient Grace and will fulfill our God-given destinies.

Matthew and Felicia built a modest one-story house in the quiet area of town far from the hustle and bustle of the central business district. The attending serenity of the area made living there worth-wile for. My father made gardens behind the house and planted various kinds of fruit trees in it. The garden brought him closer to his traditional farming roots and mother nature, and he tended it with the utmost care.

Growing up I remember playing different fun games with my cousins and spending most of my time with aunties Rhoda and Vivia and Bolab, my half-sister. My parents threw their home open to many relatives who lived with us, and diligently pursued their education relentlessly.

Ikirun was a melting pot of religions Christianity, Islam, and traditional religion. It seemed every family had members from all of them, so festive celebrations revolved around the major events of those religions to this day. Christmas festival is however as the biggest celebration then Islam' Eid-el-fitr. Ikirun's traditional religion celebrates the river goddess in fetish processions that featured masquerades of different colors, dancing, and the weird practice of adherents lashing one another with whips. It is reputed that each time they celebrate the river goddess, it is always a raining day. As kids, this meant lot of travelling, receiving and visiting friends and relations. Most wedding ceremonies and burial of the departed elderly are targeted around these festivals, and it makes for much merrymaking around the town.

At the community level, religion was never used as a tool of separation or oppression. Everybody cared for one another, and hard work was respected. True success was obvious to everyone. Age was an undisputed yardstick for seniority and respect, and, of course, wisdom was associated with age. Each family had its hierarchy, and all members of the family knew where they belonged in the scheme of things. Society was quite orderly at the town level; it was like everybody knew each other or at least knew one person who knew the other.

From an early age, I understood the role education plays in the life of any person who has it in a community. More than anything in the world, I wanted to be educated. Even before I was of school age I was exposed to the rudiments of learning. One of my father's relatives who lived with us at the time was a teacher at a primary school in Ikirun, and every morning, he took me to school with him. This made me look forward to starting school. I got my chance the day I turned six. I loved learning and I understood quickly. My teacher in primary one was very impressed and never ceased to commend me for being such a brilliant student. My parents' motivation also influenced my interest in becoming literate.

My father's name, Matthew, was not a household name. He was not a world-acclaimed inventor -- not a Faraday or Einstein. He was never one of the world's richest men like Bill Gates. Yet, like these men, my father proved that success can be achieved if desired. No matter the challenges or adversities that stand in one's way, so long as one's mind is made up and one knows what one wants and is ready to make the necessary sacrifices, one will achieve his goal. Matthew did not allow opinions of others to stand in his way. Neither did he lose himself in the maze of mediocrity. He discovered his purpose and pursued it. He made a niche for himself in the heights. From him I learned that choices we make yesterday will affect the generation to come. This man's life and achievements taught me that there is no limit to what a man can achieve. All he needs is lots of determination, hard work, and a belief in himself. His limits will reach far beyond the skies.

"Every great man was once an ordinary man."—Anonymous

Chapter 2

THE GROWING-UP YEARS IN IBADAN

Matthew was a religious man who believed in God. He and his wife (my mother) attended church services regularly. My father had a church organ, and he loved to play hymns on it for us. He once told us that his father, Jon Alba, had worked with the African Church Mission and had expressed the desire to have one of his children serve the church. When the opportunity surfaced for my father to do so, he readily accepted it. The African Church Mission in Ibadan needed an administrative assistant to coordinate the activities of its missionary schools, known as the Nigerian Church Schools.

We were all excited about moving to Ibadan. To us, the inhabitants of a small town like Ikirun, Ibadan was like London. We had heard so many wonderful stories about the big cities. We looked with awe at those who came from such big cities where there were nice roads and cars. We just could not wait to move to the big city, to finally see directly all that we had heard described. When the day came and we arrived in Ibadan, we were surprised at what we saw.

Although Ibadan was indeed a beautiful city, in a lot of ways it was different from what we were used to. For instance, in Ikirun we did not have to rent rooms in a house that was also home to other people—strangers we had never met before. We had lived in a whole house all by ourselves. In Ibadan, we also had to share facilities such as the toilet, bathroom, and kitchen with the other tenants. It took a while for us to adjust to living in a "face-me-I-face-you," as such buildings were popularly called. However, our new living arrangements did not change my father's strict rules and restrictions.

The house we lived in was a kaleidoscope of ethnic nationalities of the Nigerian federation. We had different tribes living in the same house such as a Hausa soldier who, strangely at that time, was not living in the barracks and the Ibos' main breadwinner, who was working with the Post & Telecommunications Department. The other main Yoruba dialects were also well represented. We had the Egbas from Abeokuta—the breadwinner for that family was also a federal civil servant—and speakers of the Ondo and Ilaje dialects, whose main occupation was with the automobile industry. The house owner himself, who was from Ogbomosho, was a police officer.

The good thing about living in the communal village was that you knew what each person was doing, and their wives were either in teaching, nursing, or trading at Dugbe and Gbagi markets, the most popular markets in Ibadan at that time. Both markets were within walking distance from our house. Walking was the major mode of transportation for most of us children, and you had to be punctual to most places you were going: one of the maxims you heard from both adults and teachers in school was "Punctuality is the soul of business."

The house was situated at Inalende, a densely populated area of Ibadan. In growing up, one would often see injustices in one shape or another. One type of injustice was for the rich to oppress the poor or for the military to oppress and harass "bloody civilians." However, in one such instance I witnessed, it was the poor who were oppressing the poor. This incident was Timothy's fight with the Nabals and the use of "Onde" talisman to put the enemy out.

Timothy was the local tailor around the neighborhood, and because of the modest income level for most people around, he usually sewed clothes for people and they would pay later. It happened that he sewed some clothes for a family and the head of the household did not pay. The tailor followed up gently with the man, but still he did not pay. One day the tailor got tired of being owed and went to see this man in the front room. Mr. Nabal was rumored to be gifted in the use of evil powers, and, generally, other people avoided him for fear of being harmed. Mr. Nabal actually confirmed this myth as he asked the tailor, Mr. Timothy, to leave his vicinity without being paid.

The tailor stood his ground and insisted on collecting his money. It was like the battle of David and Goliath, only this time the small "David" had evil powers, and the hardworking tailor was quite tall and lanky. The man (Nabal) dashed into his room, brought out a talisman, and hit him once, and the Goliath fell down writhing in pain. It's amazing how evil powers can make a big man like that fall down in pains by a mere touch of the talisman. As the tailor fell down, all the neighbors who had stayed along the corridor and kitchen area disappeared. Nobody wanted to be an eyewitness. At that time, to be a witness for the police was like putting yourself in trouble and probably in prison, for the policemen would sometimes leave the culprit and feed on you by twisting the evidence laws to extort money from you.

So nobody wanted to come forward and help the police in any matter. Usually crime victims had to consider the cost and bear the loss; otherwise, involving the police to prosecute the offender would become another source of loss, and you could not determine the extent of the extortion and harassment from the police. The effect on society was that the rich who can afford money to spare to "buy" the police were usually right—they won in "the police courts," and most of the time the case was never charged to court as the judiciary itself was another story. The court adjourned more than it sat, and the lawyers of the rich got the ears of the judge, while the poor or innocent had no chance of a fair hearing. Therefore, the golden rule was to avoid any police involvement either as a victim or a witness.

As the people dispersed, the hardworking tailor, after some time, regained consciousness and crawled away: and, with that, the debt of that family was cancelled from his books. Like every other poor and common man, the case is left for God to judge.

Image of the Military and Its Effects on Children and the Youths

One day, while we were on the assembly line in the primary school, I noticed the assistant headmaster was pulling out some students to stand aside as we were marching into our classroom. The typical school day started by getting to your class in the morning before the assembly bell rang so that you would have time to put down your metal briefcase, which contained your books and writing materials. It was called a *"portmanteau"* in those days. Then you dashed off to the assembly line. Each class would line up its boys and girls on separate lines, according to height. The headmaster and the officiating teacher usually stood in the front of the assembly line, which was on an open field within the school compound. The other class teachers would stand behind their students, checking them out not only for neatness, but also for wearing the right school uniform, body cleanliness, and proper haircut.

At that time both boys and girls cut their hair. Girls could only plait their hair when they became senior students in the secondary schools. That daily early-morning inspection ensured that you were not only prepared for the school mentally, but it started you off on a spiritual and physical pathway. The teacher led the prayers and songs while the headmaster—the embodiment of discipline and knowledge to all—usually made announcements that concerned the whole school and rewarded diligent students. Erring students were flogged openly, and their folly was announced to all.

The assembly was usually dismissed with the school band playing a smart marching song until the students entered into their classrooms. However, on this particular day, a few of us were selected to stay behind and practice more marching steps. We were told we would be representing the school at the Independence Day anniversary parade at the Liberty

Stadium in Ibadan. I had never been there before. Fortunately for me, my childhood friend and neighbor, whose name was Progress, was also chosen. One member of staff took us to the stadium. We were there first for the rehearsals, and all the marching took place outside the main bowl of the stadium.

On the actual Independence Day, someone led us to the stadium. It was awe-inspiring for me, just coming from my little town of Ikirun, to enter the gigantic stadium. I used to see the fields of the secondary modern school at Ikirun, but this Liberty Stadium was bigger than any field I could imagine. While I was still mesmerized by the size of the stadium, the almost deafening marching music came from the combined band of the Nigerian army and the police, led by a soldier who had leopard skin carefully woven into his military uniform, and was making all kinds of displays with the mace he used to control the band marching with precision behind him.

Then members of the armed forces were on parade, and the police in their ceremonials looked awesome. Most of us became spectators, instantly forgetting that we ourselves were there to march as well. One unique aspect I noticed about the military procession was the hierarchy. As soon as those on parade had taken their position on the field, the arrival of the officers went according to their ranks, the senior officers coming in after the lesser, all properly taking their positions until eventually the military governor arrived in full ceremonial dress. It made me desire to be a soldier with their colorful and shining uniforms.

The governor decided to review the entire parade on a horse and, with the parade commander, he drew applause from the entire stadium. General Adebayo was well-loved by the citizenry. The state was quite peaceful in spite of the civil war going on. We were even told that the governor sometimes drove himself around without the usual escort to see things for himself, turning up at parties and other social functions without the typical protocol.

Reflection on Life in Ibadan City

Ibadan, a city surrounded by seven broken hills, was quite peaceful and the security of lives and properties was not an issue. You could trek from one part of the city to the other, and there are also the municipal buses running to major parts of the city. The *Sketch* newspapers (*Daily Sketch* and *Sunday Sketch*) were the official papers of the government while the *Tribune* newspapers were always throwing more light on issues. So to get a balanced view you needed to read both the *Sketch* and the *Tribune* and then make up your mind.

Western Nigerian Television [WNTV], described as the "First in Africa" television station was established in Ibadan. WNTV was a household name. In our house at Ibadan, only one person had a TV, and we all would stay outside the window of their room to watch the twelve-inch black and white TV. Programs were only for about six hours, starting around 6 p.m. and stopping at midnight. The children's programs were usually between 6 and 7 p.m. when the first set of news would be read. My parents never allowed us to watch TV, so we had to devise errands or house chores that would allow us to catch a glimpse of what was going on.

As we were growing up, the music scene was dominated by Chief Commander Ebenezer Obey and King Sunny Ade; and, in school during lunch break, whoever had heard the latest songs would sing them, using his voice to convey not only the vocals but also the instrumentation that accompanied the songs. It was interesting to see how different musical instruments were relayed with the mouth. That was our type of recorder, and sometimes, by this oral transmission, the stories behind the music also followed, especially at a time when there was a perceived rivalry between Sunny Ade and Ebenezer Obey. To date, most people in our age group still listen to either Sunny or Obey or both.

The University of Ibadan Zoo was another special landmark. If your parents had not taken you to the UI zoo, you did not belong to those who actually knew the city. And at every major school break, most students wanted to go and visit the zoo so that when others were talking in school they also could say, "I have been there."

Ibadan also has a dreadful place called the Forest of Agala (*Igbo Agala*), reputed to contain a lot of evil spirits that would remind you of the story of *"Ogboju Ode Ninu Igbo Irunmole" (literally meaning "A Great Hunter in the Jungle of Ghosts")* —a Yoruba classic and cultural fiction novel written by J.F. Fagunwa. It was a no-go area for most residents of Ibadan. It also contained a dangerous river called *Dandaru* that was reputed to drown people who went there to swim. You can imagine the kind of fear we went through in our family one day when we learned that my junior brother had left school and gone to swim at the Dandaru River. He was not only punished, but his schooling was transferred from Ibadan to Okitipupa where our father had just been posted.

Of course, this forest incidentally housed the Bower's towers from where it was then possible to have a bird's-eye view of Ibadan city. The Catholic Church Mission in the city also had a large expanse of land where they built the church and seminary school. The area was home to rich and poor, politicians and technocrats in the civil service. It was a walking distance from the church and school to the street where my father's office was located. The church attracted men of timber and high caliber from all over Ibadan. It was a highly esteemed church.

Sunday was one of my favorite days of the week. I would hurriedly get dressed on Sunday morning and race to church with the speed of lightning. It was our Sunday school day. Our Sunday school teacher, Mama Wilson, was a friendly woman and every Sunday she served the children in her class doughnuts or biscuits and tea. This made Sunday's days to look forward to.

There were other activities that made going to church on Sundays a joy to me. I enjoyed watching the procession, which was usually made up of the choristers and officiating ministers. They would march into the church auditorium looking so regal in their robes. The members of the choir wore white robes adorned with blue, black, and red surplices. They were indeed a sight to behold. They looked like angels and sang in angelic voices as they led the procession. The clergymen who came after also looked wonderful in their well-sewn apparel. I always thought the bishop's robe was the most attractive of them all. It was sewn from red cloth and its hem was adorned with white ribbons.

Personally, I adored the bishop because he was quite amicable and funny. He enjoyed telling stories, and the members of his congregation enjoyed hearing him talk. He taught us some useful tips on how to live harmoniously in a polygamous home.

The church's parking lot was another place I loved to visit on Sundays. My friends and I would go to this center of attraction just so we could see the latest cars, and this would give us a hint as to who was the richest member of the church.

Most of the prominent members of the church belonged to the Reformed Ogboni Fraternity (ROF), a group that indulges in occult acts. I believed at that time being a member of the fraternity meant that one was godly. These men, despite their association with the occult, were still accepted in the church and were top-ranking officials in the church committees. They were the major players on issues that concerned the church, and in my young mind, I saw them as role models. I dreamt of the day when I would be a "big man" like them and, of course, join the ROF.

Looking back now, I cannot remember an instance when we were taught about salvation or the reality of heaven or hell. We did not even know of the Holy Spirit. Church was just a social gathering where the rich showed off the latest fashions, drove to church in their expensive cars, and were accorded all the honor and respect in the world. The poor only attended church to catch a glimpse of what being rich was all about. None of us understood what having intimacy with God meant. Our knowledge of the Bible did not go beyond what the bishop taught us every Sunday morning. Only God knows those He graciously saved.

Emmanuel Church School belonged to the church, and after we moved to Ibadan, it was only appropriate that I would be enrolled in the mission's primary school. The students were mostly children of the church's members and so things were not different in any way from what it was like on Sunday mornings. The children of the wealthy church members were easily singled out. They looked better, dressed better, and were shown special preference by the teachers.

School was interesting and I enjoyed every moment I spent learning. My class teacher, Mrs. Kemmy Adey, was a friend of my family's and she made sure I settled in nicely during my first few weeks of school. After school every day my mother would go over my schoolwork with me and assist me where I had problems. This put me way above most of my classmates academically.

Friends Were Part of Life

Victor Fillips was my best friend. He was, in fact, the first friend I made in Ibadan. We spent a lot of time together. We loved visiting the library now and then. We had so many things in common, for he was a brilliant boy himself, and he inspired me. I had a lot of male friends, but kept girls at bay. I believed that, because we were of different sexes, we did not have much in common.

That thought pattern changed when I was in primary four. I became too interested in girls. My mind was filled to the brim with dirty thoughts of me and some of the girls I lusted after. My dreams were wild and lustful, and there were times when they were almost torments to my soul. It was like being in the Garden of Eden and offered an apple from the tree of the knowledge of good and evil by the devil. This torture continued for a long time. I had erroneous ideas of having a platonic relationship with a girl. I was in primary five when I started dating a girl. Her name was Rachel, and we shared a seat in class.

I passed my primary school leaving examination and gained admission into the Nigerian church schools, Ibadan. Although I preferred Government College, Ibadan, I had to go to the mission's secondary school because of my mother's love and dedication to the church. I became friends with a group of boys, and we formed an association called *The Black Idols*. It was a socio-cultural organization, and we staged plays and organized parties. When I was in form four, I became the president of the group, and I held that position till I was in form five. We made some major impacts. We wrote and produced plays and, at one time, were invited by WNTV for a recording.

Apart from my friends in The Black Idols, I also had other groups of friends. There were some friends I called my religious friends with whom I shared the same views about Christianity as a religion. We attended church and believed in the stronger force called God, who had the power to work mysterious deeds in our lives. There was also another group who exposed me to the world of great stories woven from the fantasies of great minds such as James Hadley Chase, Denise Robbins, Nick Carter, Lobsang Rampa, and others. We built a well-knitted web of friendship based on the enjoyment we derived from the wonderful stories we read. We would exchange the latest bestselling novels and tried as much as possible to be the fastest reader in the group.

Sarah was a pretty form two student, and I liked her a lot. I was in form three then. I wanted to go out with her and so I made my intentions known one day during the games period. She accepted my proposal and became my first girlfriend in secondary school.

We would send each other notes vowing our love for each other. We also enjoyed taking strolls together. I gave her the notes I had made in form two so she could study ahead of her classmates and teachers. This helped her a great deal in her schoolwork.

When I was in form four, I realized the favors and respect I had received from my seniors were dwindling. The senior prefect took pleasure in punishing me for the smallest offense. I was suddenly in his black book. Not long after that, I found out he was interested in my girlfriend, Sarah, and regarded me as the reason he could not get her to agree to his advances, and so I had to break off my relationship with her. Thereafter, the undue punishments ceased.

Our breakup revived my relationship with Rachel, the first girl who told me that she loved me and gave me my first kiss. We had met earlier in the primary school. Everything was going fine between us until I was drawn to Rebecca. She was the lead actress in a play that was staged in school. When Rachel found out about my interest in Rebecca, she confronted her in the girls' hostel and warned her off me. This caused a major stir in the air as both girls engaged in a serious fight. It ended my relationship with both girls, and I wasn't bothered because at that time because I had started dating Priscilla, a remedial student.

Although I had relationships with these girls, it was never sexual—we never went beyond verbal expressions of affection. It was the deep love and respect I had for my mother that made me abstain from sex at that time. She had warned me time and time again to keep off girls, and I did not want to disappoint her.

Valentine's Day, or having a valentine friend, was just a balloting exercise usually conducted by the class teacher. The practice was to write out all the names of the students in the class on pieces of paper, and by ballot whoever you chose became your valentine for that day, and whatever gift you had for the person was exchanged on Valentine's Day. In those days, it was just that; other normal relationships were carried on.

Wicked Act of Rape by Secondary School Boys

One of the shocking contradictions in the high school social life was the hush-hush attitude the school had about rape. Victor and I were walking toward the bus stop on one of our outing days (days when those of us in the boarding house were given the opportunity to visit our relatives or visit important places in town). As we were walking along, we were greeted by this senior girl called Jemima. As she passed us, Victor whispered to me asking if I had heard that she was gang-raped by about seven senior boys in the school. I was dumbfounded and shocked. I turned my head to look back at her. She was walking all alone on a day like this when most people were in pairs or groups, savoring the free hours we had that weekend day to be where we liked to be. Victor continued that the gang rape on her was the second rape. The first, according to his information, was by one of the school prefects who sent for her one evening as if there was something official to do, and -- right in the dining/kitchen area of the school -- she was violated by this fellow student who had the authority of being a school official. He timed it perfectly when every other student was away from the building. I asked how she got the instruction to come to the building at such a time. Apparently the instruction was conveyed through a fellow female senior student. She was simply overpowered.

What about this gang-rape? How did it happen? I asked. Victor told me that because the first senior who abused her did not even say any loving words or make any overtures to her, she felt that if she had a boyfriend, she would not have been preyed upon like that. So she agreed to be the girlfriend of one of the senior boys. On what was supposed to be a secret date, she went out with the boy to hang out in the house of a day student who lived not too far from the school. Unfortunately, the boy had other plans and had six of his evil friends waiting, and they in turn raped her again and again.

Why could she not report them and the senior official who misused his authority? I was told that the house mistress felt that Jemima deserved it because she dressed well and that is what must have attracted the boys to her. I felt nauseated and quite grieved for her sorrows and hoped that one day she could have real closure. One of the sad consequences of this to Jemima was that she became a party animal and quite promiscuous. This shows that victims of rape can suffer from long-term behavioral maladjustments.

Another incident of rape that I heard about happened in the boarding school again. Normally girls do not come to the boys' hostel. However, on one outing day when the school was almost empty, somehow these lovebirds believed their boyfriends when they told them that they could take a trip to the boys' hostel and nothing would happen. So these two girls visiting from another school were led to one of the reading rooms in the boys' hostel, and their boyfriends betrayed them again and, in turn, raped them. This time around, since the place was near the hostel, the boys remaining heard the cry of one of the girls and called the attention of a school tutor who lived on the premises, so help came and the girls were rescued.

We were all waiting on Monday morning to hear that these boys would be expelled from school or suspended, but nothing really happened. We were told through the grapevine that the parents of the girls did not want their daughters identified with such stigmas, so they were not willing that the matter be treated officially. No police report, just treat it as if nothing occurred. This attitude toward the handling of rape continues to make the issue a controversial one. Rather than seeing it as sin in the sight of God and man, many people hold the victims responsible for their own calamities. It is appalling that some people still treat the issue of rape with levity.

Unwise use of Time?

Clearly, 1972 to 1976 were the unfocused years of my life. I used them unwisely, and to a large extent, I was to blame for all the misfortunes that followed. I spent the time I should have used studying to go about with friends, and my academics suffered in the process. My grades were poor, but this did not bother me at all. I did not try to work hard to make up for lost time. I did not have a focus on the next goal in my life. I just spent each day as it came, with no short-term or long-term achievable goals toward a career. I would wait till a few days before my exams to prepare. I barely made it through my promotional exams. This habit, however, cost me a great deal. I spent little time studying for my final exams.

My health did not help matters. I fell terribly ill. I did not realize what I was doing to myself—not until after the WAEC results were released. My whole life hit the rocks with the failure of my school leaving certificate examination in 1976. My mother wept bitterly when she heard the news of my failure. I was completely shattered, and it broke my heart into fragments to see her so sad. I resolved there and then to do everything in my power to make her proud of me.

My father did not shed a tear when I showed him my result. He was living at Ijebu-Ijesha at the time, and I traveled there to tell him myself. He expressed his disappointment in me, and his statements further slashed me deep within my heart. My father had always been away working, and he spent little or no time with his nuclear family. The few occasions he spent at home were mainly as a community leader, and many extended family members were always there competing for his attention along with the social groups he belonged to both in the church and the town. However, he was there to discipline us, which we regarded as the worst times of our lives. We looked forward to his going away again. Sometimes when he visited from his work station and went on social nights with some of his friends, he would come home drunk and reeking of cigarette smoke. He spent long hours away from home and sometimes all night, if he so pleased. He always kept us anxious and afraid. No matter how late he returned, one of us must be awake to open the garage gate for his car and let him into the house. We walked on eggshells when he was home. Yet despite his idiosyncrasies, he still managed to provide the basic needs of his family. He paid our school fees regularly and always made me remember that education was the only source of independence I had.

A Mother Is Always a Mother

My mother, on the other hand, was a strong bulwark behind me. The attention, love, and care my father could not provide, she gave with all her heart. She made our home a place to run to, a place we could always find solace when we were burdened by life's cares. She was supportive of my dreams and believed so much in me. She proved her love for me so many times during her lifetime, and I never had cause to doubt it. She bought my first suit and ensured that every year I had new clothes in my wardrobe. For as long as she lived, she gave me both financial and moral support, and it hurts anytime the thought of her crosses my mind. I never got the chance to repay her for all she did for me. I never had the opportunity to show her that I will be forever grateful for all she did for me.

I enrolled in a remedial school at Ijebu-Ijesha to retake my WAEC exams. I stopped seeing a lot of my friends, feeling that it was best that way. I wanted to make up for lost years, and now I knew that hanging out with the wrong crowd would do me more harm than good. I lived with my father, who was now a zonal inspector of education in the town. He was transferred back to Ibadan toward the end of that year, but he left me in the care of a friend of his, Mr. Roberts, who was the headmaster of a junior high school in the town.

It was the first time I would live with a guardian, and it was not an experience I enjoyed. Life in Mr. Roberts's house was hard. We ate once a day, usually *garri* [a local staple food prepared from cassava tubal*]* and *moi-moi* [a local cake made from beans]. On rare occasions, we ate pounded yam. I was not allowed to have visitors. It was also mandatory that I go to the farm with other members of the family. My mother learnt about how badly I was being treated, and she began sending me money through a friend so that I could at least buy food.

My Life in Ijebu-Ijesha and Thereafter

I met Keren during my stay in Ijebu-Ijesha. She was a beautiful girl who hailed from the ancient city of Ife. I had seen her around in school and, from a distance, admired her. We got a chance to talk after a drama presentation, which was produced by Ishola Ogunsola, popularly known as "I Show Pepper." The play was a historical play titled Efunsetan Aniwura. As we talked, I deduced from our conversation that she had also noticed me before that day. She was a shy girl who was also very blunt. I liked her a lot. We became good friends, and that friendship led to a passionate relationship which lasted for the whole time I spent in the town.

My relationship with Keren did not distract me at all, and neither did my friendship with two other students who were also retaking their papers at the school. Tyre Rightway and Adey Sholly were both extroverts, and we all hit it off like peas of the same pod. My exams came and went, and when the results were released, I passed with flying colors. My studying had paid off, and I had done what I set out to do. That was to put a smile on my mother's face.

Even after I left Ijebu-Ijesha, my relationship with Keren continued. We did not get to see each other as often as we wanted, but writing to one another bridged the gap. She spent her holidays in Jos, and when I went to check my result, she was so happy to see me. She disobeyed the school authority by not attending a special assembly that was going on at that time. Instead, she saw me off to Mr. Winner's house. That was the last time I saw her.

Having passed my WAEC exams, my next goal was to gain admission into a higher institution and work toward acquiring a bachelor's degree. I tried to gain admission into the polytechnic, Ibadan, but my plans were thwarted when my stepbrother misplaced the forms my father obtained to apply for my admission. I had to go back to college to sit for my Higher School Certificate [HSC] Exams.

I made up my mind again to keep off women and friends who would influence me badly. There was a deep longing in my heart to be pure and to do only the right things, but it felt like living right was beyond me. I just could not help doing the bad things that I did. The least I could do was break off those ungodly relationships. This decision rejuvenated my mind and body but left me without the inner peace my heart and soul longed for. There was something I wanted so much to have, and I just had not found it. I wanted so much to find it, hold it, and never let it go.

Ibadan—a Microcosm of Nigeria

As I mentioned earlier, Ibadan afforded me an opportunity to see the microcosm of Nigeria. Within the community where we lived, all the major tribes in Nigeria were represented. In the face-me-I-face-you house, we had the Obiagba family from the East, so I picked up a little Ibo language. This was quite easy, as most mothers always had to shout instructions to their children. Not too far from the Adamasingba roundabout was the Sabo community, which housed the Hausa people. Their merchandise of different perfumes and leather slippers was freely hawked by them in the neighborhood. The local gin store was managed by a Calabar woman who had all kinds of patronage. Of course we got to know the different cities where the Yorubas came from by the dialects with which they instructed their children, but the unifying language was English. Once you get into a secondary school (junior and senior high school), you are expected to speak in English, and you are even fined by seniors if you should speak in the vernacular openly.

Football, cycling, and makeshift athletic games in any open space brought the children together without any consciousness of ethnicity. Merit was known and celebrated by all. Once you are known to be good in academics or sports, the whole community acknowledged your contribution; and if you are bad, they also knew. Correction of children was also a community thing. In fact, the closest parent to an incident would be the first to rebuke and possibly punish you for any misdeed, and you only got the icing of the cake by the time you actually faced your own parents.

I remember an incident when I was about seven or eight years old. A cigarette-like chewing gum had just been introduced to the market, and I wanted to have some. I went into our house and, from my mother's purse, I took a three-pence coin and then went to buy some gum. On my way back to our house, a neighbor's daughter saw me and raised the alarm that I had so much money and gum. Her mother came out, collected the gum and the change from me, and asked me where I got the money from. I told her it was my mother's money.

She asked, "Did she give it to you or did you just take it?"

I retorted that I just took it, since it was my mother's money. She then told me that was stealing and escorted me to our house where, by now, all the other tenants knew of my atrocity. That day the gum was confiscated, I was scolded, and my mother told me that if I take any money that is not given to me as mine, it is stealing, which is an offence to both God and man.

Later on I realized that the house owners who build in the same area are usually from the same tribe, even though they do not discriminate in lending it out for rent. This means you could actually take the map of the city of Ibadan and see the settlement pattern based on the house owners who had come from the same areas. I also saw that the trend in choosing a house of worship, either the mosque or the churches, was also based on the ethnicity of the minister in charge of the place. This explains why in our family we passed by Saint Savior's Church in Ekotedo and went all the way to Ebenezer Cathedral at the Ogunpa area of Ibadan. The Savior's church was dominated by the Egbas (people from the Abeokuta area of Nigeria) while the Ijebus and Oyo dominated the Ebenezer Cathedral.

I was living in Ibadan during the period of the civil war, and three mild things gave the semblance of war going on in the environment; otherwise you did not really see the effect of the civil war in Ibadan. Occasionally, the soldiers in their army fatigues would do exercises very early in the mornings so their footsteps and songs reminded you that some soldiers were at war. Around the Okeado areas, they built a road bunker on the major road and said that, in case of a bomb attack, it could serve as a shelter. It was never really used, so the awareness was not there. It was only in the newspapers that you got the report or update of the war, and it was also in the *Daily Times,* which featured the update. Otherwise, the other newspapers covered what was going on within the states. I remember that the Igbo families usually listened more to their transistor radio. Of course, the trend then was also to listen to Radio Nigeria, which later transformed to FRCN and, even later, to the British Broadcasting Service (BBC) and Voice of America (VOA).

Electricity and water supply were never regular in my growing-up years. It actually looked like the supplies deteriorated year after year. So reading was done mostly in the daytime, when you could see naturally. You had to use the lantern or candle once night fell. Household equipment either had battery or kerosene as alternative sources of energy.

Initially, there was only one TV station in Ibadan, which happened to be the first in Africa (as it was stated earlier). The programs were generally from 6 p.m. to 12 a.m. We children were not allowed to watch the TV; you had to be reading your book. However, in the neighborhood only two families had a TV, and you had to be there early to get to sit on the floor or a standing view by the windows.

Standing by windows to watch was the indicator that made me realize I had grown into puberty. As we usually pressed around and on each other to watch from the window, there was this night when everybody was milling around the window and Lydia was also struggling to get into a vantage position. At one point, her body was pressed into mine, and after some minutes I noticed I was sweating, not from exhaustion, but from something that had been triggered in my body.

*"Instruction in youth is like engraving in stone." – Moroccan prover*b

Chapter 3

THE DEEP SEARCH FOR GOD

Things were coming up for me. My grades improved. I wanted to become another Rotimi Williams, [a great lawyer in Nigeria], and felt good knowing what I wanted to do. Socially, I was also doing fine. I had become the president of the Historical Society of the school. It was a title I loved and it made me dream bigger dreams such as one day becoming the president of Nigeria. My new position gave me a sense of responsibility and a new view of myself. It was a turning point in my life. I even began to have close friendships with females without any strings attached, and that was something I had thought could never happen in my life.

Others things about me had also changed. My search for fun and adventure had heightened. The friends I hung out with took me to another world, and we sometimes partied amongst the big boys and girls of Ibadan. Some of the parties we attended were organized in big hotels in the town such as the Lafia Hotel, Premier Hotel, and Chrisbo Hotel.. When King Sunny Ade came to perform in Bodija, a suburb in town, we were in the crowd cheering him on. I had also developed new habits. I drank stout and other imported alcoholic drinks and I smoked cigarettes. Rothmans was my favorite.

During this period of my teenaged years, I became someone totally new. I was overly confident and so full of myself. I was daring, in every sense of the word. I proved this when I had a clash with one of my teachers who had openly punished me because I broke the school's rule by wearing the wrong color shoes. I vowed I would get my own pound of flesh from Mr. Omi. I knew he and Dorcas, a student, were dating and so I went after her, wooing her until she agreed to my advances. Mr. Waterflow, however, called me later on and we chatted and made up. I was totally satisfied. I had accomplished what I had set out to do and that made me feel good. I did not know what became of their relationship later.

Admission Challenge Again

I was devastated once again when I could not gain admission into the university to study law. The faculty did not accept me because my grades were too low. I knew there and then that the problem was indeed beyond me. I was frustrated and disappointed and lost the zest to live. I began to seek answers from God. I wanted to know the reason for these setbacks. I wanted to know why He was allowing me to face such torments.

My parents were equally saddened by it, and they decided that the problem was spiritual and they, in turn, sought answers from spiritualists. My mother went to a prophetess who lived in the Ekotedo area of Ibadan. This prophetess was known as *Iya Adura* [Prayer Mother] by everyone who knew her. Iya Adura, after praying for my mother, told her that I was under a jinx placed on me by some members of my father's family. She said they did not want me to fulfill my destiny because they felt that if I did, my mother would also benefit from it and they did not want that. She gave my mother a bar of soap for me to take a bath with and told her to tell me to see her so that she could pray for me.

I refused to use the soap and this did not go well with my parents. I stood my ground and said I would like to see Iya Adura myself and ask her some questions of my own. My mother made the appointment and on the appointed day, we went to see her. Iya Adura asked my mother to leave so we could talk, and after she left Iya Adura told me that God had revealed to her that I had a bright future. She further explained that I had many enemies who wanted to stop my dreams from coming true. I shared with her my desire to be close to God. I believed that He alone had power enough to fight my enemies. She in turn offered prayers to God asking Him to open the eyes of my understanding so I could know Him. She gave me a small bottle containing some kind of liquid and told me it would enable me to see and know my enemies. I did as she asked for a while then stopped after I realized that the liquid was not the answer to my problem, perhaps because I did not believe in it.

I registered once again for my HSC at the Government College, Ibadan. My father was fed up with my inability to gain admission into the university that year because he considered paying my fees for yet another exam a waste of money. He told me that he had not spent as much as he had on my academics on any of my siblings. He therefore decided not to sponsor me anymore. While I prepared for my HSC, I had to enroll only as a part-time student of the college. My dad gave me a note to take to the then secretary of the school's management board, and the secretary gave me a position to teach at St. Steven's Primary School in Ekotedo, Ibadan.

My Experience as a Schoolteacher

Mrs. Beauty Joseph, the Head Teacher of the school, was a true friend. She was a mentor to me, giving me all the information I needed to work as a teacher. I learnt how to write a lesson note, how to use the scheme of work, and other rudiments of teaching. She also taught me how to get along with the children in my class. I learnt from her that children have different absorption rates at various ages and so the teacher has to use the appropriate method to communicate with them. Working and preparing for my exams was not an easy task, and I had to adjust in doing so. I collected notes from my classmates who were full-time students and studied as hard as I could. I spent most of my free time outside of work in the college or in the library.

During the time I taught at St. Steven's, I became friends with a girl called Sharon who was also a teacher. I learnt from her that my first girlfriend Rachel died after a brain surgery. This news saddened me greatly as I remembered that the last time I saw her she looked so healthy and full of life. Through our conversations Rachel had revealed to me that she wanted to become a medical doctor. We had even spoken of getting together again. I did not know I would never see her again. I tried to find out further what happened to her, but Sharon advised me not to do so, so I had to live with the sorrow of not knowing.

I liked Sharon, but I liked Grace, her friend, even more. One of the reasons I pursued my friendship with Sharon was because it gave me an opportunity to get to know Grace better. Grace was a nice girl, and as our relationship progressed, I knew I wanted to get closer to her, but even at that young age she was already a party animal. I knew I could not cope with the high level of social life she was already exposed to. My mother did not want me to get into any serious relationships at that time, and she especially did not want me engaged to either an Egba or Ijebu lady. She sternly opposed the relationship with Sharon because she was from Ijebu-ode. To my mother, my marrying someone from Ijebu to my mother was like dining with the devil. I felt otherwise and continued with the relationship.

The Steps to God's Grace

Everything was going great. I was enjoying my job. I had a relationship with a fabulous girl, and my preparation for my Higher School Certificate [HSC] was going well. Yet with all I had, I still was not content. I had this desire for something more. There was a cry for something deeper, as deep as the depth of the sea. Unknown to me, the answer to my burning questions was on its way. One era had just ended and another would soon begin.

On February 16, 1980, I headed for the British Council office, Ibadan, to attend a program organized by the Christian Science Society. The meeting had been advertised in the *Daily*

Times, and my curiosity and deep quest for God made me go. However, I did not find the answers I sought at the meeting. Instead, I was left even more confused than before. The beliefs of the Christian Science Society were indeed off target. They talked about healing without atonement, and their presentation of the gospel was quite scientific. I needed an intimate and real relationship with God. I wanted to know Him. I wanted to be in His light, to rid myself of the burden of living as I was, contrary to His will.

A part of me shrieked with pain at the darkness that enclosed me. I was shaking with need for a chance to know this Supernatural Being. I felt pulled to Him like a child to its mother. I could not fathom this sudden torment. It later became clear to me that I needed to be reconciled with God. I knew that would somehow change everything, and it did just that when it happened. I hurried home immediately after the meeting and there found my cousin Queen, a student of the University of Ile-Ife. She had come to spend the term's break with us. After dinner that evening, she called me and read to me from the book of Deuteronomy, especially, all the verses of chapter 28. She told me after she finished reading that the Lord wanted me to live a meaningful, fulfilling life filled with His blessing. She also told me that the reason why God sent His one and only Son Jesus Christ to die on the cross of Calvary was for my sake. Jesus, she said, laid down the most important part of Himself so I could be redeemed. I had a choice, she explained. I could choose between having the blessings which would come from accepting Jesus or the curses that were the portion of those who rejected His gift of eternal life. I chose the blessings and Queen led me through the sinner's prayer.

I spoke to the Lord, confessed to Him all of my sins, and asked Him to cleanse me with His precious blood: I gave my heart and everything that made me who I was to Him. That day I accepted the Lord Jesus Christ into my life to be my Lord and personal Savior for the rest of my life, both on earth and in heaven. I experienced a peace I had never known. A sudden power flowed through me and enabled me. It was as though I had been reborn; almost like I bounced back to life. In place of darkness, light shone brightly and I became a victor and a conqueror where I had been a failure before. Health was restored to my ailing body. The frequent illness that was a thorn in my flesh ceased. Indeed I knew from that day onward my life would never be the same again. I knew I had been born again.

After I became born again, I denounced all ties with the world. I had read in 2 Corinthians 6:14 these words: *"Be ye not unequally yoked together with unbelievers: for what fellowship hath righteousness with unrighteousness? And what communion hath light with darkness?"*

I knew then what I must do. My relationship with Sharon could not go on any further. If I would grow with God, I had to make some sacrifices, and one such sacrifice would mean breaking ungodly ties. I became different from the man Sharon had known and loved.

There were things about me that she could no longer understand unless she gave her life to Christ as well. I had found God and I did not want to ever lose Him. I told Sharon all of this and we went our separate ways. I felt committed to pleasing my darling Lord. By an inner persuasion that I later realized was the leading of the Holy Spirit, I knew what I wanted to study in the university. When I bought my JAMB form, I filled in geography as my course of study and the University of Lagos as my choice of university.

After Queen left, another born again cousin of mine, Lolar, took over mentoring me. She exposed me to different Christian literature, particularly Kenneth Hagin's series. By reading these Christian materials, I did not miss reading secular novels as much. In fact, I learnt new things from everything I read. Insight into the spiritual man and the lifestyle of the new man was revealed to me. I learnt about the place of prayer and the Word of God in the life of a born again Christian. I grew closer to my Savior, and I was assured within my heart that the latent power from God which I was looking for was all mine to own. Jesus Christ had reconciled me to the Father two thousand years ago when He died for my sake. I am now an heir with Him

"Therefore if any man be in Christ, he is a new creature: old things are passed away; behold, all things are become new."
II Corinthians 5:17 (KJV))

Chapter 4

NEW LIFE, NEW EXPERIENCE

I finally gained admission into the University of Lagos, and this was the realization of a dream I had been waiting for so long to manifest. I was so happy, and so was everyone around me. During the long vacation that preceded my resumption into the university, I attended my first ever Christian conference. The meeting was an eye-opener and greatly impacted my life.

It was at this wondrous assembly that I met Dr. E.A. Adeboye. He is the present General Overseer of Redeemed Christian Church of God worldwide, but then he was an associate professor at the University of Ilorin. He, using the Word of God as his basis, exposed to everyone who attended the meeting some revelations within the Scriptures that most Christians do not even know. His teachings were power-packed, and he taught with simplicity and much grace.

It was from him I first heard that God does not take it lightly when anyone wants to hurt Christians. He taught us from the verse of Scripture which says, *"Since thou were precious in my sight, thou hast been honorable, and I have loved thee: therefore will I give men for thee, and people for thy life."* Isaiah 43:4 (KJV)

He elaborated from 1 Samuel 26:23, *"The LORD renders to every man his righteousness and his faithfulness: for the LORD delivered thee into my hand to day, but I would not stretch forth mine hand against the LORD'S anointed."* Commenting on this passage, he said that it's like stretching a finger against God Himself. He will stump them in your place. He is the giver of life and He also takes life when He pleases. Those words have made me totally secure and confident since then. I know that no power of the enemy can harm me because God loves me overwhelmingly.

I also witnessed my first miracle at the conference, and this further boosted my faith in God. While Dr. Adeboye was preaching, one of my cousins, with whom I attended the conference, was healed by the miraculous power of God. She had been suffering from a chronic backache since her university days; after she graduated and started working, it did not cease. But during the evening seminar, while we sat listening to the man of God teach, she felt a sudden snap in her back and the pain left her. It was amazing because Dr. Adeboye wasn't even teaching on healing. I learnt that day that men of God carry with them the presence of God, and once God is present, He heals and fulfills His words to all that are full of expectation.

Another man of God who influenced me in those early days was Dr. Paul Jinadu, General Overseer of New Covenant Church, who was a dynamic and charismatic preacher. The sermons he preached at the seminar organized by the Graduate Fellowship, Ilorin, built up my faith. I have discovered from listening to this man preaching that forgiveness of sin by God means that God will not remember those sins anymore. Immediately, when we confess our sins, He blots them away and forgets them. It is the devil's strategy to make a Christian feel like a failure before God. He advised us to put the past in the place it ought to be and leave it there.

When I arrived at the University of Lagos to resume lectures, I registered as a member of the Lagos Varsity Christian Union (LVCU). I spent my first day on campus at the LVCU prayer meeting that took place that day in Room 106 of the Engineering Faculty. That night I rededicated my whole life to God and handed over to Him all the days and years I would spend at the university. I believed I was where He wanted me to be, and I wanted to use the privilege He had given me.

LVCU meetings and my lectures took my time. I did not have time for anything else. I was totally determined to serve God. My friends were mostly members of the LVCU. I attended meetings regularly and was made the Bible study leader within a month of joining. I was friendly with all members of the executive members of the group which was led by Brother Willie Okay.

I also found time to attend meetings at the Foursquare Gospel Church, Yaba, with a friend, Brother Manuel Petro. I was invited to the Deeper Life Bible study class held on Mondays at Redeem Church Ebute-Metta, and this I did regularly until the meeting place was moved to Gbagada. Even after this happened, I still managed to keep close contact with the group. I enjoyed searching the Scriptures with friends like Brother Ransom Belly and Brother Akins. They taught me how to use the Bible concordance.

It was normal practice for us to sit on the rooftop of the Mariere Hall praying earnestly and listening for words from the Holy Spirit on what to share with the brethren in our Bible study class. I was learning to depend on the Holy Spirit. I had begun to see Him as my source, my lifeline, and my strength. I was only a channel through which His marvelous Word would flow. The study outlines were just materials. For them to mean something to those for whom they had been written, I needed His anointing and presence with me.

My constant need of the Holy Spirit must have meant a lot to Him. He, in turn, exposed the spiritual gift that had been sitting dormant within me. I noticed that when I spoke, the words would be what those listening actually needed to hear at that exact moment.

Dormitory Could Be Hell for Christians

I lived with some of my friends from the Government College, Ibadan. Due to some accommodation troubles, I had to share a room with them at the Henry Carr Hall. They made my life a living hell. They haunted me constantly and never stopped making jest of my newfound faith. They believed the supposedly born again Christians on campus were hypocrites.

Living at Henry Carr was like living a nightmare. Immoral acts were a daily feature within the walls of the hostel. Through the help of the Holy Spirit, I was able to disregard and overcome a lot of the things I heard and saw. There were times when I felt intimidated and, at times, I even wrapped my Bible in a newspaper so that none of my roommates would tease me. However, I remained steadfast in my belief, and a few years later it paid off. Two of the young men with whom I shared a room also chose to accept the Lord Jesus Christ.

I also discovered, as I continued in my Christian journey, that Christians, like all other human beings, make mistakes. We are different people from different backgrounds with different temperaments and various kinds of convictions and principles. When one becomes born again, all these differences do not automatically go away. The spirit man is renewed and we gradually begin to show in the physical what and who we are inside. I have found that it is never an instantaneous transformation.

My mode of dressing was termed unacceptable by many of the members of the LVCU. It was considered worldly to wear suits. Most of the clothes in my wardrobe were suits, and besides, I loved wearing suits. I looked good in them, and so I stood my ground despite the severe criticism. "What you look like outside," I argued, "is not what determines your faith. It is what is within the heart that counts." I shunned all critical statements about my mode of dressing and continued to be dedicated in my work with the LVCU. Not long after that, everyone got used to the way I dressed.

Most of Us Are Like Naomi—Anyway

Naomi was a member of the LVCU, and we were in the same department. When I first met her, I was greatly put off! Although she claimed to be born again, she did not live right. I judged her by her behavior and by those she called her friends. Most of her friends were unbelievers, and I tried many times to convince her to stop hanging out with them. The Christian community on campus did not accept her because of the way she used to dress.

I got close to Naomi and realized that we are like babies in the hands of God. One baby crawls and then walks faster than the other, but that does not make him better than the one who develops at a slower pace. The change that a born again man or woman undergoes after he or she accepts Christ has no stereotype or fixed pattern. I got an instantaneous release from sin after I became born again. Sin became a bitter pill in my mouth. I had my setbacks, but I walked with God dedicatedly, and I felt that it should be the same way with every other Christian in the world; they should all have a dramatic change like I had.

I accused Naomi in my heart of being the cause of her own lukewarmness. I refused to see her struggles. The Holy Spirit, however, opened my eyes to them. I stopped judging her and began to accept her. I accepted her flaws, her attributes, her disappointments, and even her choice of friends. I prayed for her and visited her regularly. We became close. She began to trust me and shared her problem areas with me; and I, in turn, gave her some advice on what she could do to overcome them.

Brother Willie Okay, who was an engineering student at the time, was a good friend and brother. He was always there for me when I had a problem to share, and once in a while he shared with me from the Scriptures. I learnt from him that when God commits little things into your hands, it's because He has bigger things in store for you, and that whosoever is faithful in little will be entrusted with much bigger things.

My Experience with Christian Fellowship on Campus

My involvement at the LVCU gave me little time to study, and that led to my having to repeat a whole session. Some question whether Christians can fail in school. Experience with LVCU showed that a full-time student can fail and have an additional session or more added due to some factors. When I got into the LVCU, I had a platform for the expression of my newfound faith; and, with my zeal for the Lord, I focused mainly on the spiritual aspects of life and did not even bother so much about academics. It was as if the academics were a necessary evil. I used to have long, sweet quiet times, and my personal Bible study could not be interrupted even when I had classes. I must dig deep to claim the nuggets from the Scriptures first before checking my classes and assignments. If there was a need for visitation anywhere, it took precedence over any scheduled academic timetable.

By the end of my second semester in year one, my academic brilliance could carry not me to pass all my majors. Some minor courses I did very well in, but there was one major course I must pass. Because of my disposition toward the lecturer, I was not doing well in attendance to the class.

In addition, this particular lecturer had his eye on me because he had been dating a student in the department, and this sister had just given her life to Christ. She was struggling with the issue of how to give up this relationship because the lecturer was married. I told her pointblank that God does not want His children unequally yoked together with unbelievers, nor should she be in a relationship with a married man. The new convert went to the lecturer to tell him that she personally had no objection to the relationship, but since her counselor (that was me) had denounced the relationship, she was quitting. That was a red card from the lecturer. As much as I studied and made up for the missing assignments, I had just one point less than the pass mark and that meant a repeat of the whole year because the university was still doing "Almighty June," and this meant failure in one major course meant failure for the entire session.

From then on I learnt my lessons in counseling. The counselee must be guided to own their decisions. You cannot force or instruct the counselee. The counselee must be brought to a point of enlightenment where ownership of the decision is theirs. The gospel is better preached that way.

From then on I also fell in love with my studies. I realized that I needed to show excellence in order to reach the type of people God had sent me to. So I studied hard and also dug deep spiritually to the glory of God. Initially, I could not believe that such a thing as failure could happen to me. I was under the impression that having given my life to Christ and doing His work meant that I could not fail. I was so weakened by what happened that my relationship with God began to deteriorate. I stopped praying and could not read my Bible. I no longer evangelized. I was gradually backsliding.

Brother Endurance was a great help at this time. He reassured me that my having to repeat a session did not mean God did not love me or was not satisfied with my service to Him. I rebuffed him and even, at one time or the other, insulted him; but he did not turn his back on me. He persisted, visiting me every chance he got.

Brother Willie was also there for me. It was he who made me realize that my salvation should not be circumstantial. He told me that I should never feel that I needed God only when everything was rosy. Being born again did not mean that challenges or nasty experiences would not arise. The Christian would still fall once in a while into the thorny rosebush of life and even graze his knees and elbows in the process. Those times were meant to make us stronger and build up our faith in God. He created those self-reflecting periods. He did not wipe away darkness when He made light. Instead, He gave darkness a place to reign in its time. He promises to be there when we face those confusing moments in our lives. One of His promises is found in Isaiah 43:2:

"When you pass through the waters, I will be with you; and when you walk the rivers, they will not sweep over you. When you walk through the fire, you will not be burned; the flames will not set you ablaze"

Brother Willie's words pulled me together. I encouraged myself and picked up from where I had stopped. I learnt a few things from that experience, too. It paved the way for me to increase in my service to God. I gave more than I had given before. Apostle Paul said in Romans 8:35, *"Who shall separate us from the love of Christ? Shall troubles or hardship or persecution or famine or nakedness?"* In verse 37, he answered his question and the answer was *"no."* Throughout Paul's lifetime, this anointed man of God, proved that he had not written mere words: He did as he had spoken. He served the Lord despite the adversity, sicknesses, and persecutions he faced. Like him, I made up my mind that nothing would make me turn my back from serving my Master. He would be first in everything.

My Spiritual Growth, Promotion, and More Challenges

The following year, I was elected to serve in the executive body of the LVCU. I served as the spokesman of the group. That position gave me the opportunity to meet with the executive members of the LVCU on other campuses and also the executive members of other fellowships. I served on delegations with them and rendered my help where it was needed. I visited some parts of the country and also met personally with some great men and women of God. My relationship with God skyrocketed at this time. I had new understanding and revelation of things like I never had before. I discovered some other gifts and talents I possessed, and all of these I was willing to put to use whenever I could.

Other brethren also recognized the hand of God upon my life, and I was constantly besieged with activities. I found out that counseling was one of the gifts I had much grace in. I recalled a sister I was following up in Amina Hall (one of the female halls in Unilag then). She had given her life to Christ during the academic session and was one of the converts the fellowship assigned to me for follow up. In those days, we always got a list of Christian brothers and sisters to write and keep in touch with so that they did not backslide while they were on holidays.

Eunice was one of these; she gave her life to Christ during the session but then went back home to meet an unbeliever boyfriend who was begging her not to break the relationship. My letters to her during the holidays initially encouraged her to stand a few weeks, but she was confused by the unbeliever boyfriend who told her that he also would give his life to Christ. However, nothing changed: They continued thereafter, having premarital sex and wild parties.

When she returned to the campus, in my process of counseling and reviewing how the brethren had lived during their holidays, I engaged this sister to narrate her story. It was then she told me that she had this boyfriend before she gave her life to Christ, that they had been sleeping together, and after she gave her life to Christ, she wanted him to also become a Christian. He would have nothing to do with "that born again thing," but he must be able to continue to sleep with her anytime he wanted since, in their culture, he was the first person to have sex with her, and so she kept on giving in to his demands. Inwardly, though, she did not like it. She said that even up to the time when she was coming back to the campus that week, she could not say no out of fear.

I knew this was a deceit of the enemy to keep her in bondage, and that nothing would happen to her if she said no to his sexual demands. I told her to reject the spirit of fear and assured her that we would be praying for her to break that spirit of fear. The boyfriend could not be converted by her. Only a personal encounter with the Holy Spirit leads one to genuine conversion. I encouraged her not to continue the relationship and agreed to keep praying for her.

Normally, when all students had just resumed from a semester break, the executive resumed some days earlier than the general students to pray, fast, and seek God's face for the session. As they prayed and fasted there was this heavy sense of a sin in "the camp," and a spiritual alert was sent out. When I got back to my room, I called my prayer partner, who happened to be an executive of the fellowship; and, before I knew what was going, on the sister had been called, suspended from fellowship, and told that the compromise in her life was what was causing the sense of heaviness in the fellowship. She wept, and I also felt very bad that I had betrayed her confidence in me.

After some days she called me and told me she still respected me as her counselor and friend, and then I knew she had really found grace, which none of us could give her. She has remained a strong and consistent Christian and got married to a good Christian brother who was also in the fellowship around that time. Was she the Achan in the camp? I don't really know, but since then I have increased my capacity to pray and intercede for people I am involved with. Now, if at any point someone's need has to be prayed for with another person, I have to seek the individual's permission and tell him or her why we need such prayer partners for that specific issue.

I apologized to Eunice and continued to be close to her even during the period of the suspension. I told her not to leave the LVCU. She did continue with the fellowship and even became one of the executive members before she graduated. Eunice's confession and how the executives took it as sin in the camp almost made her lose her faith. When I read about the journey of the Israelites to the Promised Land and of Achan's sin, I remembered this incident.

Balancing Fellowship Activities, Service to God, and Studies

In my part two, I was again offered another chance to serve as a member of the executive board, but I declined it. My refusal to serve that year was due to the fact that the task was enormous and time-consuming. Then I was asked to serve as one of the hall representatives: It's akin to the job of a resident pastor. I did not want my life to revolve solely around activities. A deeper, consistent personal relationship with God was what I desired. My role in the executive of the LVCU was demanding, and it gave me less time with God and less time to study. I concluded that my role as representative of the fellowship would push me farther from God. Declining the offer to serve was therefore the right decision, and I was very sure of that.

I met Israel Tade, the editor of the *Campus Mirror*, the fellowship's magazine, at the main library one day. We had seen each other at the fellowship a couple of times and were well-acquainted. That day he told me he wanted me to be a part of the valiant team of writers for the magazine. I was stunned, but I saw it as an opportunity to put my writing abilities to use, and so I obliged. While in form three in secondary school, I had worked with a stage production team and co-wrote some of the plays we staged. Although I knew I could write, I never saw my writing as a means by which God could touch the souls of others.

Israel was a leader in every sense of the word. He knew what he wanted with every edition of the magazine and did not relent until he got it. He was goal-oriented and made well-laid plans that were excellently executed within the time allocated for them. He did everything in his power to make sure that members of the team were united as one. Love was the binding force that made the *Campus Mirror* a success in those days. Being a part of the team was a joy. We were one big happy family. The editor who took over running the magazine after Israel left did not understand this, and this led to the disintegration of the team. Things have never been the same to date, but I believe the magazine can still live again and will do so someday.

One of my assignments while writing for the *Campus Mirror* was to interview Kunle Ogunde, the heir apparent of the Ogunde dynasty. It was a real testimony, and the genuineness of his conversion was visible for all to see. It made a good story, and many lives were touched by the publication of the magazine. However, I was puzzled that the elders in the faith who first counseled him after conversion told him to leave the acting and music platforms as they were the devil's media. In fact he had the best musical instruments in the country then; King Sunny Ade bought some of them off him after his conversion. To my mind, he could have been mentored by people like Jimmy Swaggart or Ron Kenoly. Somehow, the lack of mentors and people who are true Christians in all areas of life is responsible for this shortsightedness in the Christian faith. We have left so many platforms because we consider them the devil's territory.

It was in the days I spent working with the magazine that I met Michael Homestead, Charlot Oracles, Rachael Baba, Lam Moses, and later Joy Yale. I was closest to Mike, Charlotte, and Lam. We all spent a lot of time together. We went to social gatherings as a group and were called "The Writer's Family." Michael was quite close to Charlot, and we always accompanied each other to functions. We had a strictly platonic relationship. The thought of venturing into fornication never crossed our minds. Even after we all got engaged to other people, we still stayed close.

Thinking about Dating and Relationship…with Candace

I can still remember the first time I met Candace. I was sitting in Lovett's room when this young woman walked in. There was something about her that attracted me to her. I cannot say if it was the way she carried herself or the way she spoke or gesticulated or laughed. Looking at Candace that day made me want to spend the rest of my life with her. I supposed Candace felt the same way. Our friendship blossomed as we spent a lot of time together.

We were taking a walk toward the lagoon one evening when I popped the question. I told her in simple terms that I loved her and believed the two of us were meant to be together forever. After I said it, I realized the full implication of what I had done. Fear gripped me for a moment, and I felt I had done something wrong. I wanted to plunge into the lagoon and hide there forever. Candace's response was not what I expected. There was no trace of excitement in her voice or on her countenance. She told me she would need time to know if marrying me was God's will for her. It took her about nine months to give me an answer, and after that, two very significant things happened.

Not too long after I proposed to Candace, I met some other female friends and enjoyed their company a great deal. I discovered that the type of love I felt for Candace was no different from what I felt for these other sisters. For example, Eside was a friend I respected. She was an Evangelical Baptist when we met and did not know much about the Bible. I took it upon myself to minister to her about the baptism of the Holy Spirit. The pattern was to check out their Christian foundation, confirm if they were truly born again, and map out a spiritual follow-up to perfect their faith. I felt as obligated to these sisters as I was to Candace. I treated them all like my sisters.

I was always excited to see and hear from Candace, and I had spoken the truth when I told her I loved her, but I felt there was something more our relationship needed which was not there. Candace, on the other hand, could not understand a lot of things about me. She felt left out of my life; she wanted to be the most important thing in it, and I did my best from time to time to prove this to her. However, I was dedicated to some other new converts, brothers and sisters, and I had to follow them up. My axiom was "the poor you have with you always." I believed we would always have each other. The others would not always have me. They needed me for that moment, and I had to give them attention.

Another issue that arose was her parents' non-acceptance of our relationship. Her mother believed I was not good enough for her. A fellow medical student would have suited the bill more nicely because she would have more prospects with him. They could build a hospital together, giving her financial security for the rest of her life. I could not offer her the financial standing that would give her a high place in society. Due to a sincere desire for our relationship to grow, she shared all that was said by her parents and stepbrother with me. Then she encouraged me and told me what we needed at that point in time was God's strength and help. So we decided we would seek His face and made up our minds not to let anything come between us. After that, we prayed and fasted consistently and found solace in some passages of the Bible:

"Heaven and earth shall pass away, but my words shall not pass away." Matt 24:35 (KJV)

"For the vision is yet for an appointed time, but at the end it shall speak, and not lie: though it tarry, wait for it; because it will surely come, it will not tarry." Hab. 2:3 (KJV)

We worked at making our relationship work. We fixed Bible study and prayer days and went evangelizing together. We did all we could so that we could make each other happy. However, other loopholes arose. She complained I was not spending enough time with her, and she did not like the idea of sharing me with others. Simply put, she made me realize she was not cut out to be a pastor's wife, and my disposition did not help matters. I could not give up serving others simply because Candace or any other person on the face of this earth felt differently. This was my first priority. We could not come to a compromise, and by the time she moved to the college of medicine, the gap between us had grown even wider. We knew then that the relationship was not meant to be, and after years of trying to make it work, we parted ways.

While we were having our differences, I sought counsel from one of the pastors in the church I attended and he opened my eyes to a few things I did not know about relationships. According to him, for a relationship to work and lead to marriage, both parties must first be friends: "Get acquainted, and then get to know them," he advised. "Know what interests them-- their likes and dislikes. In all the time you are working on being friends with this person, put your feelings aside. Build a sincere friendship. As it deepens, things will begin to take their natural course. There will be trust and openness—those are the pillars of a foundation that will be the basis of long-lasting relationship, if indeed it is the will of God for both to get married. Most Christian singles do not know all of this; rather, they meet a brother or sister they like, they just walk up to them and make their feelings known, and the next thing you know, they are engaged and courting."

Thinking about Dating and Relationship …with Abigail

After my breakup with Candace, I took out time to think about what I really wanted in a woman. What qualities should my future wife possess? I wrote all these down, and not long after I met Abigail. She was Ijaw, from the southwest part of Nigeria. She fitted the description perfectly. It was almost as if I had known her before we met. I believed I had met the ideal mate and she saw me in the same vein, but our love and desires could not make the relationship work. Abigail's guardians did not approve of our relationship. My being from the Yoruba tribe (western part of Nigeria) made me an outcast, and they threatened her until she was afraid and intimidated.

She began to compromise because she felt more obligated to her family than to me. Although she did not share any of this with me, her actions spoke for themselves. She traveled to Kaduna in the northern part of Nigeria on holiday and spent months there, only writing to me three times. While I just could not shut up about our relationship and told every single friend about it, Aminat kept it secret from everyone we knew. I knew there was nothing I could do. The center cannot hold when both parties do not have a mental understanding about what they want, and so we broke up.

Thinking about Dating and Relationship …with Sarah

I reasoned that the best way to actually know who I should marry was for the sister to come up and make a proposal to me; that way, I figured, the love would be in existence in the relationship. Not long after this secret prayer and desire, Sister Sarah approached me and told me that God spoke to her saying that we should do His work together. I interpreted it to mean assisting me in the assigned pastoral responsibilities I had then, but as events started unfolding, we began dating and she was in the lead. It was a relationship that seemed to be in the fast lane, and before long she had concluded marriage plans with her family, and I was just being informed of dates to work with. I chickened out because I did not have any personal conviction that God was in any of these activities. So, for the third time, I was out of a relationship.

Relationship and Marriage: the Way I Perceive It

I was heartbroken and devastated. The love I had given sincerely had been thrown back to my face. Why did this always happen to me? I questioned God until I did not have any more questions to ask. There were brothers who held the view that my failures in relationship happened because I was not praying hard enough to receive God's will for me. I did not agree with them and still do not agree. I have learnt from experience that marriages can be likened to how one gets saved. Conversion comes via various routes. One man meets God on his sickbed at the age of fifty while another gets born again in a prison cell at the age of fifteen. Yet another is born into a home where Christ is preached; and, from the cradle, he knows Christ and grows up and naturally accepts Him. God does not work in a pattern; He does not use the same blueprint for everyone. He has plans for each individual; and, when we understand that, our lives become less full of worries.

When some people meet their spouses, immediately they feel a witness in their spirit, and it all works out. For others it doesn't work that way. But that does not mean it will never work for them in marriage. It does not mean they do not seek God enough. Quite to the contrary, it means that God has a plan for them; and, when the time comes, He will reveal what He has in store.

"It's not over till it's over," a common slogan says.

Don't wait for the right person to come into your life. Rather, be the right person to come to someone's life.

--Unknown

Chapter 5

WORKING IN THE MINISTRY

In my final years at the university, I knew where the National Youth Service Corps would post me to serve. I had a conviction that my primary assignments would be with the Foursquare Gospel Church in Lagos, Nigeria. The Lord had shown me through a scripture that this was His will for me. Matthew 13:44 says, *"Again, the kingdom of heaven is like unto treasure hid in a field; which when a man has found, he hides, and for joy thereof goes and sells all that he has, and buys that field."* This scripture spoke to me that I should invest my NYSC service period for God, and I knew what God wanted of me.

He further confirmed this by speaking through one of His children, Sister Nancy Okiki. As long as it was the Lord's directive, I rested assured that He would bring it to pass. Some of my friends attributed my desire to remain in Lagos to the fact that I wanted to be near Candace, my ex-fiancé. I did not bother to argue or try to convince them otherwise. I just let "sleeping dogs lie" and awaited the manifestation. When the posting was released, I was posted to Imo State. I was not shaken, and I did not go to the orientation camp in that state; I confidently remained in Lagos. I lay the whole issue before the Great Shepherd. I was fully persuaded in my heart. He took over and the whole issue was promptly resolved. Through the follow-up of Brother Remmy Lawrence in the church, I was posted to Lagos to serve within its walls.

I was disappointed the day I started work at the church. The church administration office had no proper orientation program outlined and so I did not have a job schedule. I was dismayed by all of this, but the Lord assured me that it was all part of the plan. The Holy

Spirit would be my reliable guide. With this assurance from the Lord, I did not relent in my efforts. I invested quality time, energy, and resources into the work of the ministry.

Testimonies of God's Faithfulness

I worked with the Telephone Counseling Ministry (TCM) because that was where God directed me to be. Every day I would sit by the phone and wait for someone in distress to call. I would then sit back and counsel them and reassure them of God's love and help. It was a serious task indeed since the lives of others were involved. I constantly asked God to help me speak His words to the people who called and prayed that, through the words, they would find salvation and the testimonies they earnestly desired. God made this a daily happening in the TCM. He proved Himself faithful each day. The testimonies that followed were so many that, if documented, they would fill countless pages.

There was the case of the young graduate with Higher National Diploma [HND] who called one day. He wept bitterly as he shared his ordeals with me. He was always feeling inferior whenever with his peers. He thought every other person was better than he. He was on the verge of committing suicide because life had no meaning for him anymore. I spoke to him and led him to Christ. We said some prayers together after this. Seven days later he called to testify that the prayer had indeed been answered. He was gainfully employed.

I also remember the frustrated housewife who had found out her husband was cheating on her. She was broken-hearted and deeply hurt. She was counseled to fight the battle by being civil. Instead of nagging him, she complimented him. She cooked his meals and took great care of the way she looked. Her house was more welcoming and homey. She stopped being pessimistic about her marriage and even forgave her husband. God worked a miracle in that home. Her husband forsook his mistress and paid more attention to his wife. She gave her life to Christ and attended church with her children and her erring husband. He eventually gave his life to the darling Lord.

There was also the woman who was healed of many years' affliction of yellow fever and the man who was instantly healed while I was still praying with him over the phone.

The testimony of how Ruby was saved from committing suicide one night is also remarkable. She was fed up with life after a series of abuses and decided to take an overdose of sleeping tablets; she used a newspaper to grind the pills together and sprinkle them into a drink in order to commit suicide. As she did so, her eyes caught the advertisement of the TCM with the helpline number requesting that people not give up but dial the phone number listed instead. She called, holding the deadly powder in one hand and the telephone in the other.

In our conversation, she told me how she had gone to her bank to transact business. A bank clerk, who initially appeared helpful, decided to charm her using diabolical means to control her. He instructed her to give her personal details including where she lived. Later that day, the bank clerk came to her house and actually moved in, starting a series of sexual, physical, and emotional abuses. He brought so many charms to her house that she became a captive in her own home. For a few moments she did regain her senses, but fear that the man would kill her and her daughter made her continue to suffer in silence for quite some time. Days translated into months, and she decided she could not take it any longer. She was a senior business executive who lived in one of the government reservation areas of Lagos metropolis.

She called around 9 p.m. that fateful day, and after rebuking the spirit of suicide, I prayed with her and asked her to come over to the church that night. When she came, by the grace of God, I allayed her fears, and I told her to go back home and sleep in peace. I arranged a deliverance team the following day and went with some brethren from the church to pray and physically remove the charms and amulets this man had planted in various corners of her house. Somehow, I finished counseling and it was quite late for me to go back home, so I decided to stay over in her guest room.

The following morning, the team scheduled to follow her up came by, and when the team leader was told that I had stayed in that house overnight, she went back to the senior pastor of the church to report me for disregarding the rules of the TCM by visiting a counselee without authorization and also spending the night there. Consequently, I was suspended from office as the minister in charge to allow for further investigations.

The following Sunday when Ruby came to give her testimony in church, I was no longer in charge; she was handed over to another counselor to follow up. Somehow, she got confused as to what was really going on and stopped coming to church. I was told by the church not to contact her again, and I felt that the process was not properly handled. However, it gave me an opportunity to see firsthand how church discipline is meted out.

A committee was set up to investigate my handling of the case, and by the time the various members had taken their turn to ask me questions and other brethren who did not know what really happened started hearing half-truths, the whole scenario looked bigger than the corrective measure of keeping a balance between a male counselor and a female counselee. It showed me firsthand which brothers only cared for me because of my office, as some did not greet or regard me while I was on suspension.

One or two people did more than give mere words of caring; they actually sought me out where I was living to pray with me and bring me some groceries. This experience gave me an early opportunity to learn how to relate to people as a person and not necessarily through my office. By the time the committee finished, the soul won had been lost, and I was recalled from suspension and actually elevated to work as a pastoral assistant in the pastor's office.

God healed the sick and repaired broken hearts. He comforted the hurting, provided jokes, and restored the sinners to Him. Along with the other counselor, I dedicated my time working at the TCM and went back every day singing praises to the Lord. He proved Himself able through those controversies.

Another Gracious Privilege in God's Service

I also got the opportunity to serve as coordinator of the Lifeline Ministry. When I first started working, and coordinating correspondences, I never dreamt that God would put the overseeing of the day-to-day administration in my hands. It was a great privilege indeed. My desire for expansion and innovation in that ministry was fulfilled. The members of my team and I watched as God increased the ministry from one slot on LTV8 (Lagos State Television) to two slots on Radio OYO (Oyo State Broadcasting Service) and one slot on OSTV (Ondo State Television). God was meeting the needs of men and women all over the country through the church's television and radio teaching programs. We had a hard job following up the converts that were reached through them.

The job was taxing. I weighed sixty to sixty-one kilograms when I began working with the church, and by the end of my service year I weighed only fifty-four kilograms. We had to spend so much time in the church, and it was not devoid of troubles or failing, but we always went home every night praising God for testimonies. I enjoyed every minute of the job—so much so that my desire was always to be occupied working for God. One of my greatest personal joys at the Foursquare church was the warm relationships I shared with everyone there. I learnt a lot just by working with counselors on various shifts.

I also understood from the various seminars and workshops that the church leaders organized for the various arms of the church. The telephone, TV, and counseling ministry were like the elite corps of the church. So we had the privilege of getting seasoned speakers who were not only spiritual but also shared their practical Christian lives. One example of such real-life sharing was done by Prof. Tokunbo Adeyemo, then the executive secretary for the Africa Evangelical Association, who told me he went through three different courtships as a Christian before eventually getting married to his wife.

By the time I was listening to his testimony I already had my cup full of my three experiences as a Christian, and I knew then as I still know now that those experiences were to ensure that, once I got it right, my marriage, by His grace, would be a success. It has been quite shocking at times to hear of brethren who had perfect photo-finish courtships—men who were spiritual giants—whose marriages hit the rocks. I thank God for people like

Professor Adeyemo who could open up and give somebody like me the hope of "go and sin no more" as I was just recovering from the ashes of breaking a third engagement with a sister I had thought would do the work of the Lord together with me. She was great and had her own ideas of how the home should be run, many of which I did not share. Rather than trying to save my reputation, I opted out, knowing it was better than getting married and filing for separation later. Details of what I have learnt from these various life experiences on marriage will be shared in another book.

Programs and Revival Services: Benefits and Challenges

One other spectacular feature of the National Headquarters church was the Annual Renewal and Revival services. It was always good while the services lasted, and the challenges I have been privileged to look at from the insider's perspective are issues such as the question of attendance figures before and after the revival services. Of course, during the meetings, the attendance would be high, but one week after, people usually went back to sleep and waited to be woken up in another year. Very few anointed speakers justify the return on investment, and then you can see the figures and the spiritual growth go upwards.

Sometimes you get an unbalanced teaching that for the next quarter keeps you doing damage control through Bible study and sometimes the general Sunday school time. I believe it is better to follow the leading God has given you for the assembly and faithfully carry out that divine assignment rather than to engage in the popular programs of doing jamborees for the sake of tradition. It's puzzling at times to see a new ministry that is less than six months old organizing revival services rather than teaching the basic doctrines that will make them stand. Somehow the attraction of making flyers and posters to announce the church does not allow us to properly wait on God for what He wants the church to do.

Another issue I have noticed is that, too many times, we glamorize conversion and make the new converts instant celebrities that go from one church to the other. At the end of the day, because they have not been properly followed up, they go back to the world and the body of Christ is not impacted positively.

Rev. Olu Farombi, the general overseer, gave me wonderful spiritual and moral support during that year. I learnt from him about the importance of the Holy Spirit in the life of any minister.

Dr. Onuzo was a loving senior friend in the Lord. I personally adored his frankness and open-mindedness. He was also a true leader who understood the importance of teamwork. I respected and loved him and always had confidence that if he embarked on any God-given assignment, it had no choice but to work.

Brother Hunt's humility and preparedness to learn drew me to him. Brother Victor and his wife were very sincere. Through our daily interactions, I found that they were a couple worth emulating.

Rev. Dr. Badejo was, and continues to be, a source of inspiration to me. Despite his workload at the then Mitchell's farms (where he worked in those days), he still had time for the work of the Lord. I was greatly challenged by this. It was from him I formed the habit of praying and studying the Word before going to bed every night. I also learnt from him the principles every successful man knows and observes, making the best use of each day. I spent nineteen hours working and five hours resting and this helped me during the youth service year.

Service Year and Life Ahead

During my service year, I had some indelible experiences from which I gleaned vital lessons. The snares of the devil were laid before me, but God gave me victory.

He also provided miraculously for my needs. I was staying with a Christian couple in Ikoyi during those months. I lived in a single room at the boys' quarter. Before I moved in, I did not have a single possession. I sent my younger brother to our house in our hometown to bring back some kitchen utensils and furniture, but my father sent him back empty-handed with a message that said, "You do not take anything out of my house. As a child in my home, you are supposed to bring furniture and kitchen utensils to equip the house."

Papa Charlie, who I had met during my days as a writer with the *Campus Mirror*, asked me if I needed anything. I told him what I needed and he gave me a single iron bed and the other amenities that made my single room home for me throughout my stay there. It was like a dream when in 1986 all the corps members were called up for the passing out parades. That signified the end of our one-year contract with the Nigerian Youth Service Corps. I left the TCM and the mantle fell on Brother Yemmy.

Power Tussle at the Foursquare Headquarters Church

One of the challenges I faced growing up as leader in the body of Christ was to find out that not all the spiritual principles of the Bible are strictly followed in leadership. While I was at the University of Lagos Christian Fellowship, there was no leadership tussle or manipulation. Brother Wale Oke led with a transparent leadership style. Everybody knew what was to be done, who was in charge, and everything was done accordingly. So when I got to the Foursquare church, I was expecting a higher flow of that type of leadership. I was shocked when I began to see that some leaders were manipulative and wanted to get into the pulpit by any means. Sometimes they used unsuspecting church members to play church politics just to get fame, and I did not know early in my Christian life that there were some lucrative postings and people would curry favor of whoever was in charge to get posted to those assignments. What I also later realized was that when they got to such positions they did not have the unction or the anointing to carry out the assignment and they ended up as a misfit—or their ineffectiveness became so apparent that with time they had to be changed. However, this is usually at a cost of some members leaving the organization or incidents happening before it become clear that it was not God's choice.

Sometimes people lobbied to be posted as pastors to some churches, but rather than experiencing growth and spiritual victory, the opposite of that was experienced until the church council began to pray and start the whole process with the leadership again.

The Career Path—Search for the Job

After my NYSC period with the church, I was offered the position of assisting minister in Foursquare Gospel Church, Yaba, in 1985; but, somehow, when I prayed on it, I was not led to accept it. As a full-time minister, I wanted a platform like my mentor and great leader Dr Samuel Odunaike.

I made up my mind that I was going into the personnel management field, too. First I had to get professionally qualified. I enrolled to be a member of the Personnel Management of Nigeria and started taking the exams. I did not get a personnel job straightaway, so I started with a teaching career at Science College, and before too long, a door opened to join the Personnel Department of the Nigerian Airports Authority.

While I was there, I was able to go back to the University of Lagos for my master's degree program. After I completed the program, I felt that the private sector was much better than the public service, which appeared to me to be stagnant and uncreative. However, I enjoyed the profession of human resources management. It has helped me to have the skills to quickly identify people's potentials and put them on the right path toward fulfillment. As I continued my relationship with God, I realized that the mandate He had given me to help people fulfill their God-given destiny was also relevant to my profession. Having put my feet on the personnel career path, I moved closer to my mentor and leader both in the church and at home. In addition, through spiritual impartation and professional guidance, I became a better professional human resources practitioner. Later on God brought this mentor my way in several areas of my life.[3]

---

[3] Dr Samuel Odunaike *http://www.dacb.org/stories/nigeria/odunaike_samuel.html*

Some Christians Are Not What They Profess to Be!

Stepping out of the church to work as a teacher, a public servant, and a personnel manager gave me the opportunity to see life from a non-believer's perspective. My initial thoughts were that, as a Christian, I should only be friendly with people I identified as Christians. So at first I did not really interact with my "worldly" colleagues. I sought friendship only with the Christians and had my triangle of church, workplace, and home. Nothing else came in. However, I began to realize that those of the world did actually pay attention to me, and some of them were more sincere and straightforward than certain Christian Brothers I knew. For instance, I held one of my elders in church in high esteem, and unknown to me, he was living a double life.

A Christian does not drink any form of alcohol or have extramarital affairs; and, if you are not yet married, there is no sex before marriage. When we were in social gatherings, I initially just put in an appearance to help them say the opening prayers and then left the place immediately. The way it was usually done was for the Christian to say the opening prayers and a Muslim to do the closing prayers or vice versa. I usually got to do the opening prayers as a Christian, and then I disappeared. Later on, this elder would ask me why I didn't date another lady and have a feel for what sex is all about and not wait until the wedding night as we Christians believe. My answer was always, "The Bible does not permit such, and God will not be happy with such a fellow who breaks His laws." Some years later, I found out this elder had a parallel home apart from the Christian home we in church knew. So I later understood where the pressure was coming from.

I also got to know of another senior friend in the faith who would travel out of his station on official assignments. Since he was not known there as a Christian, he would use it as an opportunity to date other women and then come back as if nothing had happened.

I also learnt of a sister who was so naïve she accepted a dinner invitation with a top executive in his hotel suite and went to bed with him after the dinner. She was not initially bothered by the incident since nobody else knew, but sometime after she had returned from the official trip, she realized she had missed her period. Then she started praying to God for divine intervention. And that was her first time having sex--just one night!

I later realized that by being transparent to my worldly friends, they were drawn to my faith as they saw my struggles and challenges and the way I sought to find God-given solutions. I remembered an instance where the security personnel attached to my office came to inform me of how the other managers were fortifying themselves with charms and I needed to do the same. I told him NO, and some years later when he was fired from his job he came to me for prayers because all his protection could not save him.

"Your calling is to be faithful to God where you are, and in doing this all work is sacred, spiritual, and worthy of your full attention and energy. When you get to work, you are not entering a secular environment as much as you are bringing the sacred into the world by following Christ wherever you are."

— Joe Thorn, Note to Self: The Discipline of Preaching to Yourself

Chapter 6

O DEATH, WHERE IS THY STING?

She lay on the bed, looking more beautiful than I had ever seen her. Her eyes were closed as though she was asleep, and her scarlet-ribboned lips, which had uttered so many words of caution and encouragement, and given me so many smiles, were now clamped together in silence.

"Call her name," the nurse instructed me. "Perhaps she will hear you."

I whispered her name into her ears, and, for a second, she muttered something as though she heard me. Her eyelids even fluttered, but she slipped back again. My cousin Double tried to call her name, and he too failed; she remained in a coma, helpless and dying.

During the Easter break, I had come home from the university where I was studying to spend the holidays with my family. I was so shocked to hear that my mother had been admitted to the hospital. I went to see her, and the doctors told us that she had fibroids in her uterus, and they had to be removed for further tests. The operation was successful, or so we thought.

I saw my mother on Easter Sunday and we talked. I even introduced her to a friend of mine I had met at the hospital who was a doctor. She asked me to help her wipe her back, and I did. After propping her up, she told me to take care of my younger ones and tell my father she appreciated all he had done for her. I never suspected that would be the last time she spoke to me. Later that day, when I got back to the hospital, we were told she was in a coma.

I could not believe my ears. There I sat, not sure of what to expect. I tried to stay positive. I envisioned her coming out of her coma and smiling at me again. I waited for that moment, and others who loved her waited with me. My father sat by her bed day and night. Like the rest of us, he believed, paced, and hoped for a change. Every chance we got, we all would join hands and whisper prayers to God telling Him to help us get through this. We woke up on Easter Monday and believed in our hearts that the risen Lord would heal her. We arrived at the hospital and did not see her on the bed. The woman with whom she shared a room told us the bad news. She had passed away the night before and the nurses had carried her corpse away. My father was summoned to the doctor's office immediately. When we arrived, we sat in the main lobby, weeping bitterly.

I saw my mother again that day. The nursing sister pulled off her covering cloth, and I gazed at her beautiful face, which was asleep in death. No more would I hear her call my name or feel her touch me or see her weep, laugh, or smile. She would not attend my wedding or know my wife or see me graduate from the university or even hold my children in her arms. My mother was gone to be with the Lord forever, to stand before the great Judge of all men.

Many years later, I researched the thief that had deprived me at that early stage of my life from having that delicate flower with me always. It had robbed me of the opportunity to accomplish for my mother all the things I had so wanted to do for her. I sat opening books and Bibles, reading through verses, and looking for answers about this joy spoiler-- death. My quest led me to the highest citadel of learning, the university. Among those who expressed lofty opinions and thoughts on the subject was a professor of philosophy and logic, a guru and a genius, a man of many parts. He was amused at the subject of my research but gave me all the help I requested. "Death is a known fact in logic and philosophy; the good and the bad, the clean and unclean, the atheist and the Buddhist and the Christian, you and me, sir, will all die and this completes the circle of life," he said.

Before then, I was not aware that death was such a comprehensive subject of philosophy. I found some of the revelation disturbing. I listened with rapt attention as the professor expatiated. I appreciated his contribution and got so much more insight about death than I had before I visited him.

On a further study, I realized that the wise King Solomon had documented truthful parts of his assertions about death in the Bible:

"For the living know that they shall die: but the dead know not anything, neither have they any more a reward; for the memory of them is forgotten. Also their love, and their hatred, and their envy, is now perished; neither have they any more a portion forever in anything that is done under the sun" Eccl 9:5-6 (KJV).

I can say with all boldness that the Bible is the best existing authority on the subject of death. It teaches that man will eventually return to his eternal home (heaven or hell) after his physical body has been returned to the dust. Hebrews 13:14 emphasizes that man is a pilgrim here on earth. The Bible also reveals to us another glorious happening, that death has been conquered by the Lord Jesus Christ:

"For this corruptible must put on incorruption, and this mortal must put on immortality. So when this corruptible shall have put on incorruption, and this mortal shall have put on immortality, and then shall be brought to pass the saying that is written, Death is swallowed up in victory. O death, where is thy sting? O grave, where is thy victory? The sting of death is sin; and the strength of sin is the law" 1 Cor 15:53-56 (KJV).

And so death was no longer an enemy lurking in the dark. The resurrected Lord has given every believer victory over it:

"Verily, verily, I say unto you, He that heareth my word, and believeth on him that sent me, hath everlasting life, and shall not come into condemnation; but is passed from death unto life" John 5:23-24 (KJV).

"And it shall be said in that day, Lo, this is our God; we have waited for him, and he will save us: this is the LORD; we have waited for him, we will be glad and rejoice in his salvation." Isaiah 25:9 (KJV).

"Therefore will I divide him a portion with the great, and he shall divide the spoil with the strong; because he hath poured out his soul unto death: and he was numbered with the transgressors; and he bare the sin of many, and made intercession for the transgressors." Isaiah 53:12 (KJV).

Jesus, who had not sinned, died for the sins of the world. His death on the cross brought an end to the power of sin and death in the lives of everyone who believe in Him and accept Him. The mystery of the cross had performed the great victory over death, Satan, and demons.

"The thief cometh not, but for to steal, and to kill, and to destroy: I am come that they might have life, and that they might have it more abundantly" John 10:10 (KJV).

Death is a word that puts shivers down the spines of many people. They do not feel comfortable mentioning or thinking about it. It represents darkness and fear and separation from loved ones eternally and, of course, judgment. It is ironic that everyone wants to go to heaven, but nobody wants to die. They say, "Why talk about something awful when there are other interesting topics we could talk about? For example, property…that's a much pleasanter topic."

And this point of view has been carried into the church. Pastors feel comfortable teaching about wealth acquisition and have successfully swept the message of death and eternal life under the carpet. Instead of discussing ways to save the souls of the dying, we talk about church growth, organization, and unity.

My mother died while I was still struggling to get a financial footing. I was in my part two at the university, and it hurt to lose her, but I felt consoled and glad when I remembered that she gave her life to Christ prior to her death. Death did not really conquer her; instead she conquered death.

Folks,

Let us not neglect the weighty matters before us.

Let us not push evangelism aside;

Let us not sit back and watch our neighbors, brothers, and sisters tread the path that leads to hell.

Let us not pass over the urge to tell them about the death and resurrection of our Lord Jesus.

Let us inform them about the barrier that has been removed.

Let them know that our sins, which caused the estrangements between man and God, have been cleansed, forgiven, and forgotten. Therefore, death cannot keep man and God apart.

Let us pursue the things of the kingdom, living holy lives both in secret and in the open.

Let us prepare earnestly for the coming of the Lord. No man owns tomorrow and so it is therefore dangerous to live unwisely.

Death need not be a terror anymore. It should instead be a reunion with our Lord in the heavenly place where He sits waiting for the return of His precious ones who looked death in the face and conquered. O DEATH WHERE IS THY STING?

There is an essential difference between the decease of the godly and the death of the ungodly.

Death comes to the ungodly man as a penal infliction, but to the righteous as a summons to his Father's palace.

To the sinner it is an execution, to the saint an undressing from his sins and infirmities.

Death to the wicked is the King of terrors. Death to the saint is the end of terrors, the commencement of glory.

—Charles Spurgeon

Chapter 7

FINALLY, THE MATCHING RIB

I was through with my service year and wanted to marry. I had been looking forward to getting married within the next two years but things did not go the way I planned. There were days when I was forced to believe that I would never meet the girl of my dreams. I feared that I would have to spend the rest of my life alone. But God had no such plans for me. He had assured and reassured me that the woman He created for me would come, and when she finally did, it was worth every minute of waiting. I finally understood how Adam felt the first time he laid eyes on Eve. I let out a sigh of relief at the sight of her. Olutoyin is beautiful, charming, and very hospitable. I was content beyond measure because I knew the waiting was finally over.

In His Own Time, He Makes All Things Beautiful

Toyin's Story

[The following is my wife's account of our early relationship and courtship.]

I had not meant to snoop. I cannot remember what drew me to the letter on the table, but I was drawn to it. I read it and then read and reread the words, clutching the paper tightly in my hands, unable to believe what I was reading.

"I still love you."

The letter was signed by some lady, or so I thought, called Adewumi. How could he? How could he do this to her? I paced around the room disturbed by what I had read. Uncle Akin was engaged to Sister Arin, a nice, lovable girl. I respected and liked her a lot, and the last thing I wanted was to see her hurt. I had thought Uncle Akin felt the same way about her and could not believe that he was secretly involved with some other girl.

This is so unlike him, I thought. I decided I was not going to just sit back and watch Akin break up a wonderful relationship. Arin was the perfect match for him. I had to drum that fact into his head before it was too late. I sought out my uncle and, when I found him, I tongue-lashed him, waving the letter before his face so he could see I had proof. He was greatly amused by my behavior and laughed at me. After he calmed me, he told me that the writer was a friend of his and that he was a male. I was flabbergasted.

"But the words … the words he wrote," I stammered. "They sounded so tender and filled with much emotion. How can a man write in such a manner?"

He shrugged in response and that ended the conversation. I was relieved that Arin and Akin were still in love and put the incident behind me.

A month later I met Adewumi in person. The encounter did not have any great effect on me. It definitely was not like in the movies where a girl meets a boy and their eyes connect and bright lights pop up around them and they just know they will be together forever. My uncle introduced us when Adewumi visited him at our house. We talked and became friends afterwards, and it could not have been helped, as he gradually became a part of the family.

We were close. He shared his problems, dreams, and aspirations with me and we would talk about them. I listened to him and enjoyed talking with him. We did not see each other from late '86 to early '87. I was preoccupied with getting a medical degree at the Ogun State University and barely had time for anything else. Although I did not see or hear from him, thoughts of him would cross my mind, and I would pray for him.

In May 1987 he was invited to give a talk in my school, and I was glad to see him after such a long time. That reunion gave us a chance to revive our friendship. Although we did not get the opportunity to talk like we wanted that day, we were able to fix a date to do so. I invited him to Sagamu and we had a terrific time together.

We kept in close contact after that meeting. He would write me beautiful letters with enchanting and encouraging words. I loved reading his letters. It did not cross my mind at this time that he had feelings for me; neither did I think he was the ideal husband for me. My friends who read the letters he wrote to me felt differently. They believed there was more to the nice words Adewumi wrote me and that I should read between the lines. I refused to see what they saw and would always shout them down, telling them over and over that Adewumi was just my friend and nothing more. They did not seem to agree.

On Adewumi's birthday that year, my dear friend Solly Adeg suggested I bake him a cake, and I did exactly that. I took it to his house where I presented it to him. What happened afterwards left me wondering if my friends were not right after all. He introduced me to his family as a special friend, and when it was time to pray, we all prayed together like I was a part of the family. I felt uncomfortable with it all but kept it in my mind. While he saw me off to my uncle's house that night, Adewumi talked to me in a manner he had never done before. He was tender and more openhearted than he had ever been. I listened to him as I always did. That night I sensed from our conversation something I had never sensed before; and like Mary, the mother of Jesus, I kept all I had observed within my heart and pondered it.

I had been praying to God for a partner for months, and I remembered that each time I prayed, I would always end with these words: "Lord, in Your time, make me willing." I did not know why I prayed that prayer, but the Holy Spirit always brought it to my mind and made me pray it. Between 1984 and 1987, five brothers had proposed to me and I, by the leading of the Holy Spirit, courageously told all of them no. They always came back, insisting on their convictions, and I in turn always turned them down.

On August 15, 1987, I attended a program at the Foursquare Gospel Church, Yaba, in Lagos. I saw Adewumi that day, and he dropped me off at the motor park so I could board a bus back to Sagamu. On our way to the park, he told me he would visit me on the 29th of that month. He roused my curiosity when he said that he had an interview with a certain "medical personnel." I did not understand what he meant by that, but since he did not explain further, I left it at that.

On August 18, I was sitting on my bed studying for my exams when I heard the voice of the Lord say to me, "Put aside your books and praise Me." I did exactly as I was told. In the middle of the praise session, God spoke to me and I wrote down all He said. These were His words to me: *When He, the Spirit of truth, is come, He will guide you into all truth; for He shall not speak for Himself but whatever He shall hear, that shall He speak and He will show you things to come ... He shall glorify me: for He shall receive of me and shall show it unto you.* " John 16:13-14

"Surely, the Lord God will do nothing but reveal his secret unto his servants the prophets." Amos 3:7

"Behold, the former things are come to pass and new things do I declare: they spring forth, I tell you of them." Isaiah 42:9

"But ye have unction from the Holy one and ye know all things. The anointing which you have received abides in you and you need not that any man teach you but as the same anointing teaches you all things and is truth and no lie and even as it hath taught you, you shall abide in Him." John 2:20-27

"There is an establishment, yea, there is a foundation. The time has come. The appointed time is near. I the Lord have spoken; that which I have purposed shall I bring to pass now.

You shall be glad for I am your salvation and foundation. I will lift your head. I will help you. Do not be afraid or dismayed. I am with you. ADEWUMI shall come and he shall speak my counsel. I shall go before you and I shall be your reward. I am the Lord that calleth you, and near you shall I stand forever."

He ended, but not after speaking this mystery: *"This love shall grow. It shall not wax cold. It shall yet be replenished for I am the source of it. Look to me and to none other for I, the Lord, am your strength and refuge. He that calleth thee is faithful. Men shall love you, yea, favor they shall show to you. You shall be a treasure, a wonder in the sight of many, for I shall arise upon you and you shall shine."*

And this warning: *"Remain you faithful; keep that which I have given into your hands. Walk in my counsel and obey at all times. I will help you readily."*

And finally the admonishment: *"Just trust. He that trusts in me shall not be ashamed. ADEWUMI is your man."*

I was surprised and troubled by what God had said to me, but I felt peace flow through me like I had never felt before, and I knew that, indeed, it was God. I understood why He started out by giving me four verses of Scripture before He spoke. I had, at a point in time, stopped praying to God for a life partner. I had made up my mind to wait until he came before I prayed to God to know if indeed he was the perfect will of God for me. I guess God understood me and wanted me to believe what He had to say, and He had to reassure me about all of it for indeed these words sounded so unbelievable.

Two days later He spoke again. This time He taught me certain things about righteousness. He employed me to have a right standing with Him, and to do this I had to…Love the truth and peace (Zechariah 8:9); Do what you know is right (Daniel 4:27); And the word of righteousness is gentleness and assurance forever (Isaiah 32:17). God said it was only when I did what was right that I would have His peace. I had to stop worrying and bothering myself, He said. He admonished me to love so I could attract His peace. I discussed all that the Lord had said to me with my best friend, Bolla Sol, and her fiancé, Charles Adeyanju. They assured me that they would seek the face of the Lord on my behalf, and I know they did.

On August 29, Adewumi came as planned. I had decided to tell him that I wanted our friendship defined since I could no longer understand what we had. I had also planned to tell him to stay away from me. Before I could get the words out of my mouth, he told me the Lord had told him the name of the lady he would marry and that he promised himself he would not mention the name to anyone until he was sure.

I was taken aback by his words, and within my heart I thought, "Oh God, did You hear that? He knows whom he is going to marry. What in the world made me think it was I?"

Then suddenly, from nowhere else but God, a great peace filled my soul and I looked him in the eyes and asked, "So, could you tell me where that sister is at the moment?"

He looked at me, obviously amused and amazed -- at least I deduced that much from his stare -- and I stubbornly refused to answer. Instead he threw another bombshell by asking me straight out, "Has the Lord told you anything about me?"

I was surprised he asked that question and bluntly refused to answer it. He told me afterwards that God had shared some passages from the Scriptures with him, which he wanted to share with me. One of these passages was from Proverbs 12:28: *"In the way of righteousness is life and in the pathway thereof, there is no death."*

He explained this to mean that God was in agreement with our friendship and it made him so sure that we would always be friends. That day Adewumi and I parted as friends, but I knew the matter was not resolved.

I saw Adewumi again. This happened when I traveled to Lagos after my scheduled exam was postponed. Adewumi invited me to visit him on the 21st of that month, and I accepted. Well, as the day drew near I began to fidget. How could I have accepted his invitation? I tried to think up reasons why going to Lagos on the appointed day was improper. I finally made up my mind that I would not go. I convinced myself over and over again that I had made the right decision. I wrote a letter to Adewumi telling him I would not be coming to Lagos as I had earlier promised, and I also told him as politely as I could that since our relationship was not defined, I did not think it was proper for us to see each other.

I gave the letter to my Uncle Akin, who was traveling to Lagos that day. Immediately I noticed that my peace left me. I felt a struggle in my heart. I spent so much time in prayer after this asking God to restore my peace, and each time I prayed He replied in a gentle voice, *"Toyin, you have to go to Lagos."* This went on for days. I was terribly confused. There were days when I lay before God pleading with Him to spare me and allow me just to disobey Him, but He whispered to me these words: *"Toyin, My thoughts toward you are thoughts of peace and not of evil, to bring you to an expected end."*

I shared my troubles with Bolla, and what she told me surprised me. She said she felt a burden in her heart to pray for me and she did. After praying she heard God say to her, *"Do you imagine that I would lead Toyin astray?"*

Those words touched my heart. It made me know once again that He was mindful of me. Before she could utter another word, I told her I thought it was only right to obey God and so I was going to go to Lagos to see Adewumi. She smiled. On my way that morning, I told God these words: "Lord, let him be in Lagos when I get there, and let him be expecting me." The Lord patiently reassured me over and over again.

When I got to Lagos, I went straight to Adewumi's house. He wasn't home but left a note on the door letting me know where the key was. It was as though he knew I would be coming over and this amazed me once again. I was hungry and decided to prepare lunch.

When he got home, he met me in the kitchen and did not seem in the least surprised to see me. After the meal, he sat me down and told me everything God had told him about me. He told me God had chosen me to be his wife, he loved me deeply, and he wanted me to be his wife. As he spoke, I felt peace within me and I was not afraid at all. I knew in my heart that this was my place of rest. I did not accept his proposal that day. I told him I would seek God first in order to know His will for me.

I already knew what God felt about it all, and on the 24th of November, 1987, He once again reassured me with these words: *"I am in it, your relationship. I founded it, it is of Me. Let not your heart be dismayed. Let it not be afraid for I am He. I am true. I stand and establish; I shall be by you. With Me you are safe for I am He that called you to yield to Me a great thing that is rewarding. You shall be glad for I shall make you glad. None can stand against you, but shall be for you; with you I stand; with you I will be. All is well, Toyin my dearest, all is well. I will lead you alright not to be slaughtered."*

On December 9, He spoke yet again saying, *"Today will I confirm to you what I have said and you shall know that I am He who said I shall instruct thee in the way you should go; with Mine eyes will I guide thee (Psalm 32:8). I am the Lord that changeth not. When a thing is of Me it stands, and I tell you it shall stand for I shall be thy fortress thereof. Run unto Me and you shall be saved, none shall be able to stand against thee, for I am the founder of it all. All that thou hast feared, I have heard and known, and they shall not stand."*

Later that day He proved His word through a very unlikely vessel. One of the brothers who had been persistently proposing to me visited me and shared with me Job 23:14: *"for he performed the thing that is appointed for me and many such things are with him."* The words took my mind back to what God had said that morning, and I was indeed surprised at the person God used.

On December 11, 1987, I did not intend to go to Lagos, but I really missed Adewumi and wanted to see him. I prayed to God to know if it was okay with Him and His response was positive. I arrived in Lagos on the 12th and the next day I accepted his proposal—and that's a decision I have never regretted. I can still boldly say with all my heart, soul, and body that I love him and will always do so. God is indeed true. When He says He will do a thing, believe He will. He is not a man that He should lie.

Adewumi's Story

When I met Aduke Olutoyin Adebusola Onafuwa in 1984, I did not think that she would one day be my wife. There was however something magnetic about our meeting. She is beautiful, charming, and intelligent. She reminded me of the sixteen-year-old girl in *The Sound of Music* movie (and I still call her my Sweet Sixteen). There was a kind of mutual friendship between us; her uncle, Akin Oyegunwa, was my good friend and he often spoke of her. We hit it off the first day we met, I liked her and she liked me, and we became good friends. Due to my friendship with Akin, I became close to the family and treated Toyin as a younger sister and a reliable prayer partner. We spent time together and enjoyed each other's company. She was trustworthy, zealous about the things of God, and eager to learn.

By the time I began to seek God's face concerning the right woman for me, He whispered her name into my ears, and whenever such thoughts of who to marry crossed my heart, I initially hesitated because I felt she was too young for me and knew too much about me already to accept me with my experiences with other people to whom I had been engaged. However, God thought differently. For several days I kept hearing the same name, and God confirmed it in various other ways.

On August 26, 1987, Oyin and Mike, two of the friends I had made from my days at LVCU, had to spend the night with me because their flight was cancelled. The next morning, before they boarded the plane, Mike shared three verses from Jeremiah 33 with me. Through those verses, God ministered to me again and answered the many questions I had put before Him about His choice for me. This was the beginning of a series of confirmations that led to my proposing to Toyin.

On August 29, I visited Toyin at Sagamu for a prearranged meeting. I realized for the first time on that day that I was falling in love with her. I shared with her the same verses of Scripture the Lord had impressed on my heart to share with her, and this included Proverbs 12:28. I also remember telling her that day that God had told me who my wife was, and she tried to make me tell her, but instead I asked her if God had told her anything about me. This she refused to answer.

Having received God's choice for me, I told my family members about her and asked them to pray with me before I proposed and they did. I also spoke to her uncle, Akin, of my convictions and intentions. He also took time to pray and raised no objections. The Ajibosos and Efunwapes were good Christian friends with whom I also shared what I felt because I respected their judgment. They prayed with me and felt convinced also that I was making the right choice. Even with these convictions and confirmations, God further reassured me by giving me infallible proofs.

Toyin was scheduled to come to Lagos on November 21, and I planned to propose to her when she came. I was still getting ready for her visit when Akin arrived a day before and told me she would not be coming as planned. I did not know what to do at that point, and once again, I shared with Akin what convictions I had received from God and also my intentions of proposing to her. Akin told me she had asked him to give me a letter, but he could not find it. I knew then that God was at work because Akin was never known to be careless.

The following day, after praying, I was convinced in my heart that, in spite of her earlier decision, Toyin would still come. I asked God to do me some special favors as a confirmation of His leading. I told Him that if she did not come that day, I would forget the whole issue and continue with my life. I further told Him that when she came, if she was the right woman, she should help me clean the house and cook a meal.

Though it was a Saturday, I had to go to the office, clear my desk, and pick up a manuscript of a book for Dr. Badejo, who is my spiritual leader; so I left a note for her telling her where the key was. I was delayed for a while by Dr. Badejo's secretary, and when I eventually got home I found Toyin right where I prayed she would be: in my house cooking a meal! After the pleasantries, we settled down to talk. I asked her if she wanted to know who God had chosen to be my wife. She did not reply but that did not put me off. I proceeded to share with her all God revealed to me about her, and I told her I loved her and wanted to marry her. After I finished she told me she would like to take time out to ask God for further instructions on the matter. She said what had guided her so far in her friendship with me was the peace of God which followed every instruction He gave her. I assured her that I would remain her friend regardless of what response she gave me.

Despite the fact that her response was not what I expected, I knew that telling her how I felt was the right decision, and God confirmed this through other signs and witnesses. On December 12, 1987, after twenty-one days of thorough consideration, Toyin agreed to my marriage proposal and we commenced courtship.

It was at the Annual Conference of the Personnel Management of Nigeria, held at Enugu, that I later had the opportunity to tell my mentor, Dr. Odunaike, about whom I wanted to marry; and as I had earlier desired, I wanted him to be either the minister that joined us together in holy matrimony or the chairman at the wedding reception. He agreed to do either of these roles, but informed me to let him know the actual dates because of his tight schedule. Mr. Oba, who later became my father-in-law, had observed that some church activities were going on in his house. These activities were actually coming from his church and I was included in those activities with the wife of the senior pastor. Mrs. Rachael Odunaike, despite being a wife and senior minister in the church, still had the time to follow up and bring some people to church regularly from Ikoyi to Yaba church. My wife-to-be was one of them. The Odunaikes also hosted the church life center in their house, and being a leader in the church, I not only attended but also assisted in the follow-up of the neighborhood activities of the church, which included visits to my soon-to-be in-laws' house—Mr. Oba.

Interestingly, as our wedding approached, my father-in-law rejected the idea of his coming to our church for his daughter's wedding and decided that we would go to his church. Since he was the father of the bride, he would also choose the wedding chairman. By the time he approached Dr. Odunaike to come and chair his daughter's wedding reception, it was a prophecy fulfilled.

In his counseling before and after the wedding, he prophetically told us our home was being set up by God to fulfill a particular mandate in the body of Christ for this end-time move of God. He declared to us that, as the psalmist of old lamented that the godly man ceases, so also are godly homes diminishing. Our home therefore must be a restorer and reformer of homes according to God's counsel.

"I am my beloved's and my beloved is mine."

-Song of Solomon 6:3

Chapter 8

AFTER THE VOWS

"Dearly beloved, we are assembled here in the presence of God and before this congregation to join this man and woman in holy matrimony. Marriage is a holy estate instituted by God and commanded in the Scriptures as honorable to all who enter it lawfully and in true love. It is confirmed by Christ's solemn words and hallowed by His presence at the marriage feast in Cana of Galilee and is declared by the great Apostle Paul as signifying the mystical union between Christ and His church. Therefore, it ought not to be entered into lightly and wantonly but thoughtfully, soberly, and in the fear of God daily considering the case for which it was ordained…

"Firstly: marriage was ordained for companionship…

Secondly: marriage was ordained for procreation of children…

Thirdly: marriage was ordained so that the natural instinct and affection implanted by God in His creatures should be hallowed and directed aright, that those who are called of God to be His holy estate should continue therein in pureness of living…

Into this holy estate of marriage, these two young people come now to be joined. Therefore, if anyone can show just cause why they may not be lawfully joined in holy matrimony, let him now speak or forever hold his peace. I require and charge you both as you will answer at that dreadful judgment when the secrets and motives of all hearts shall be disclosed that if either of you know of any impediment why you may not be lawfully joined together in marriage, please confess it now. Know for sure that if any persons are joined otherwise than God's Word allows, then their marriage is not lawful..." This the officiating minister read to Toyin and I, on our wedding day.

Adewumi Writes...

It was a perfect day for a wedding. The weather was fair. The morning breeze was cool and soothing to the skin. Toyin looked so beautiful in her dress. I was stunned at how beautiful and wonderful this woman I was marrying was. I knew there and then that I would not have wanted to say those vows with anyone else. Yes, as I saw her walking down the aisle I knew the vows were meant to be shared with her and no one else.

The wedding ceremony was quite elegant, and God's glory radiated through. It was everything we dreamt it to be except that our Pentecostal ministers were not allowed to officiate along with the orthodox Methodist priests. They humbly seated amongst the congregation. We stood before the officiating priest and heard the charge and exhortation. Then we declared our undying love to one another before our friends and well-wishers who gathered for the ceremony. I promised from my heart to love, adore, cherish, and honor Toyin for as long as we both shall live, and I meant every single word. She looked in my eyes and spoke those words to me, and at that moment I knew I was the most favored man in the whole wide world.

Toyin Writes...

It was a beautiful ceremony, though simple—well organized and one of the loveliest days of my life. It ended in a most surprising note. My husband had booked a suite at the luxurious Ikoyi Hotel and we would be spending our honeymoon there. There I was, all that time thinking we would be returning to our two-bedroom apartment after the reception, which was filled with well-wishers from both families. It was indeed music to my soul to know that we would have our first night together at a place as enchanting as Ikoyi Hotel.

I felt good and highly esteemed at the new dimension of love and respect that filled my heart for the young man I had married. I looked forward to unraveling the mysteries of our love daily for the rest of our lives together. The other mysteries within him were just waiting to be unwrapped. The suite was tastefully furnished and beautiful. Ikoyi Hotel was indeed the perfect honeymoon spot, but we did not rush to satisfy our natural physical desire (and there was indeed a longing to reach out for each other). Instead, after putting down our luggage, we knelt down and held hands and praised our Lord and Master who in His appointed time had made all things beautiful. We thanked Him for everything He had done, especially for bringing us together, and committed to Him the unknown future. We knew that with Him we had nothing to fear.

I was so happy and did not find it difficult to give myself to my husband on our wedding night. I gave the totality of my spirit, soul, and body, honoring and adoring him with them.

I have never regretted accepting God's choice for me. No other man would make me feel so complete or understand me like Adewumi. Despite the storms and trials we have faced through the years, God has irreversibly bonded our spirits, souls, and bodies together. Each day has remained heavenly for me. God daily fills our lives with new wine that never dries, and to Him eternally I will be grateful for this wonderful gift of love He has given me in the person of my husband, A. Adewumi Alabi.

Adewumi's Charge

I believe marriage is a consecration between a man and woman who will forever love each other to honor, cherish, and adore; to have and to hold, in good or bad, sickness and health, in sorrows and in joy, for better and for worse till death do they part.

The wedding day is a celebration of memorable events. The ceremony always leaves everyone who attends thinking about the beauty of love. The bride in her beautiful dress glowing like a diamond, the words of promise the couple say to each other, the exchange of rings, the music that brings tears of joy and dancing, singing and jubilation—all these are just the beginning. After the last drop of wine is drunk, the last morsels of cake are swallowed, and the guests have all gone home, then real life begins. The couple begins to run the race, and it is not always a pleasant journey to embark on. On the road are thorns and thistles. Of course there also are beautiful, sweet-smelling roses of all colors and green pastures that spread for distances. Sometimes it is all sunshine and a perfect day to travel while on other days "it rains cats and dogs" and the road becomes treacherous. There are so many uncertainties, and that is why it is advisable to travel this road with the guidance of the One who ordained it. He drew the blueprint at the Garden of Eden. He understands everything about the road because He created it.

"And the LORD God said it is not good that the man should be alone; I will make him a help meet for him" Gen 2:18 (KJV)

He knows every bump, every turn, and how the end of it all will look. Giving Him the reins means sitting and enjoying the ride; that is a decision you can never regret. We have a lot of break-ups in our world today because many couples get married for all the wrong reasons. They make beauty, success, wealth, fame, position, sexual gratification, and character the yardstick for choosing their life partners. These parameters are sands and structures built on sands shall surely collapse.

Sadly, that is what is happening in so many marriages today. The divorce rate is at its peak. Many children are deprived of having a stable and loving home. This lack of guidance ultimately contributes to children turning their grievances onto the society, becoming menaces where they should be mentors. They also walk the same paths their parents trod and leave their own children regarding marriage as a plunge into hellfire.

The best decision any single person can make is to let God lead him/her in choosing the right partner to marry. Knowing that this man or woman is indeed God's choice for you is the best way to start out. Even when imperfections show their faces, you are not moved because you know that this is God's gift to you. His thoughts toward you are of good and not evil. Even when the storm rages, they will eventually be still because of the presence of the Master in the boat.

As a husband and a father, I have learnt a lot of things. I have made my share of mistakes, but I have also discovered from my blunders some vital factors that would help not only my marriage and family life, but also those of many others. These I'll happily share with you. Firstly, I manifest love and self-control in dealing with my wife. Secondly, I try to protect my family's dignity and personality. Also, I make sure that my family and I spend quality time together. We pray, eat, and do other useful activities together. The only time that does not happen is when something inevitable comes up, such as an official assignment.

Doing things together binds us together. We talk about the kind of day we had at work or school; we share opinions about various issues; and we get an opportunity during our family altar to pray about the things we need in our house. Furthermore, I do not allow pressure from the ministry or office, friends, or parents to influence my family life negatively.

I also make it a matter of principle to always tell the truth to my wife and children anytime I am wrong. That way, they always trust me. Husbands, there's a lot you can do to make members of your family feel happy and secure always. You need to exercise patience and tolerance in all situations. Never forget the vows you made that beautiful day to that woman. "I take thee … to be my wedded wife, to have and to hold from this day forward, to love and to cherish till death do us part, and to thee I pledge my troth."

Amazing, isn't it? Amongst the billions of women on earth, you chose this one woman and did not bat an eyelash for one minute when it was time to speak those words to her in public. That only shows that no matter what differences you two might have, you can still make it work. Just lay it all before God and let Him lead. He has the perfect solution for all problems.

For with God nothing is impossible. Luke 1:37

Toyin's Charge

Marriage can be likened to a seed. Within it is the branches, roots, leaves, and, of course, tasty fruits; but one can never tell all this by looking at a tiny seed. Not until it is put in the ground and the seed begins to mature are the many things which are hidden within it revealed. The tree grows tall. Its branches spread far and wide and become a refuge for the birds and squirrels, and the tasty fruits satisfy the hunger of man and beast alike. However, it all began with a tiny seed.

As it is with the seed, in marriage each day new behaviors are revealed. Sometimes you wonder to yourself "Is this the man I married?" Some of these behaviors you like: others, you do not. How can you, as a wife, make marriage work despite the occasional conflicts and unpleasantness that will arise? How can you, the mother and wife, make your home a peaceful pleasant haven for your husband and children? Well, making Jesus Christ Lord in my home has helped me a great deal. With Jesus Christ, we had a perfect example to follow. We allowed the Holy Spirit to lead us in every issue that arose between us.

Communication is vital in any relationship and especially a marriage. My husband and I love to talk, and he does it excellently. We have no communication gaps in our home. We believe in clearing issues, and we do that by talking about them no matter how difficult they are. We might not always agree, but we are able to make our views known and that way we can reach a compromise. We also apply this method with our children, and it helps in the house. If talking is important, listening is doubly vital. Sitting back to listen to what your spouse has to say makes it easy for him to trust you, especially if, after hearing him talk, you do not turn around and nag or criticize or ridicule him. It gives him a sense of belonging to know that he can be heard.

I love listening to my husband talk. I am never in a hurry to get my own opinions across, and when I eventually say what I think, he respects my judgment. Whatever he wants to share whether it's good or bad, he knows that I will listen to him contently. This act of listening pulls us closer together.

Occasionally, the table turns and a crisis arises. We may experience a clash of wills. I want things my way and he wants his; this is inevitable in marriages. You both will not always agree. This is, however, not an indication that the marriage relationship is not working. Rather, it is a path that leads to harmony, consequential love, and perfection. Minor marital conflicts need not be destructive. Through them both spouses ought to learn they should work on making their relationship last always.

I have learnt from some of my clashes with Adewumi that when one wins and the other loses, the relationship loses. We both win or lose together, and knowing this should boost my motivation to make our marriage win. What I think or do not think, how angry I feel or do not feel, should not matter one way or the other to me. What should matter is breaking the barriers and jumping the hurdles and claiming the prize, which is a happy marriage forever.

A colleague once asked me how I got along with my in-laws. Well, I would say that I have been blessed with in-laws who are nice and loving. But like other relationships, we have had our share of setbacks and shortcomings but have overcome them in the end. I have committed my in-laws in the hands of God and allow God to lead me even when the air is charged between us. I simply trust Him to resolve the problem. With Christ, I have learnt to win it all for it is written in His Word that I am able to do all things through Christ who strengthens me.

Wives, it is also important that you try as much as possible to avoid persistent argument. Learn to leave your defense to the Lord; after all, He is the foundation of the relationship. Instead, submit yourself to your man.

"Wives, submit yourselves unto your own husbands, as unto the Lord. 23 For the husband is the head of the wife, even as Christ is the head of the church: and he is the savior of the body." Eph 5:22-23 (KJV)

When you submit to your husband, he will give you love and honor in return. You will enjoy intimacy in your relationship. You can only have what you give. If you have a man who is quick to flare, then understand his moods and try to avoid doing those things that will bring out the worst in him. I must say here that I am grateful to God for giving me a very warm, loving, and understanding husband. He has deep respect for my feelings and is not put off by my flaws. Adewumi is never bossy. When I have to work on the nightshift, he takes care of the house and never complains of the toll my very demanding medical profession takes on our family. Rather, he accepts all of me.

Over the years he has stood by me through the most difficult times. For instance, when I was pregnant with our son, the devil kept tormenting me. I constantly rejected those evil imaginations against me and my child by using the Word of God to counteract them. My husband stood by my side like a brick. He encouraged me and did not stop praying with me.

My baby came earlier than expected. Fortunately, I had gone to the hospital for my routine checkup when the doctor ordered that I should be wheeled to the labor room. The most important part of it was that my husband was by my side through it all. He held me and whispered encouraging words into my ears as I pushed our first child into the world. He was there to watch our baby take his first breath. That moment is still precious in my memory and little gestures like that have only endeared my husband to me and made me love him even more.

Perhaps you are not having as wonderful a time in marriage as I am. Well, I believe that it is not over for you. I believe God can heal the wounds in your marriage and bind your family back together again. But it will not just happen because you believe it or say it. It will happen if you are ready to make sure it works. Make a sincere dedication and commitment to make your marital life work. Submit where you have been heady and overbearing. Your home should not be a battleground, nor should it be the place where you express all the jargon you learnt about women's liberation or feminism. Submitting 100 percent to your husband does not make you a slave. Sarah submitted totally to her husband Abraham. Submitting keeps your home peaceful and your marriage blissful. So which do you think works best, God's way or your way? You decide.

"God intends and expects marriage to be a lifetime commitment between a man and a woman, based on the principles of biblical love. The relationship between Jesus Christ and His church is the supreme example of the committed love that a husband and wife are to follow in their relationship with each other." ~ John C. Broger

Part two

Chapter 9

FROM CLEAVAGES TO CLEAVING

Relationships are not always easy, especially when deception is at the root of the relationship. This can happen even in Christian marriages.

Mark and Leah have been married for over two decades and, on the surface, they appear to be the perfect, ideal couple. They have been through a lot of struggles together in their careers and in raising their family. They both are committed Christians who had accepted the Lord Jesus Christ as Lord and Savior at an early age and both had courted each other in a Christian courtship. Both were Christian leaders in their church organization. They both resolved at the beginning of their marriage that they were going to cleave together, having realized that as God guided them to each other, they were meant for each other. They planned to continually trust God to bring to pass the manifestation He had promised their home.

One of the foundational truths they shared with us in relating their experience is that they both came from families where their parents, grandparents, and great-grandparents had always divorced each other. Polygamy and marital infidelity have always been part of the family heritage. They felt like they were the chosen ones who would to bring an end the corruption of an ancestral line that the enemy seems to have targeted from the beginning.

With all these revelations and resolutions, you would think that this knowledge would have kept Mark out of marital infidelity, but it did not. Worse still, till several years later, he did not even realize he was living a deceptive double life. Self-deception had set into his life and, because he did not realize this, his dangerous personality and character flaws almost destroyed his marriage, home, and the lives of his wife and their lovely children.

Mark loved the Lord and sincerely believed he was called of God to be a minister. So he always plunged himself into activities that were church related. This involvement, along with his knowledge of God's Word, made him become a leader in his church, and he was quite distinguished at his career in his work place as well.

Since childhood, Mark had always been troubled about sex. He grew up being sexually abused. However, he did not realize it was an abuse and never sought help. As a growing young child of about five or six years of age, he recalled being sexually abused by the nannies and aunties that were helping taking care of him while his parents both worked outside the home. His dual life started from this infancy. He was quite brilliant and intelligent and liked by everybody around him. However, he was also shown improper love by his cousin who secretly continued the abuse, and Mark grew up thinking all that was love, too.

This led him to continue to have two sets of friends: those who continued to challenge him to succeed academically and those who drew him to moral compromises. These friends also introduced him to the secrets of pornographic materials. By the time he gave his life to Christ and came in association with more of Christians in the college campus where he studied, all those sexual desires were suppressed and they only re-surfaced after graduation as he started his working career.

As a result of his earlier abuse, sexual temptations always plagued him. Twice, before his marriage, but during his engagement to Leah, he had fallen prey to prostitutes while on business trips.

Mark's involvements with other women were mostly conducted with utmost holiness and a very high sense of integrity and that made Leah feel secure that she was getting married to a dependable and reliable professional who feared God. His secretary at work could attest to his honesty and that he turned down advances and other temptations from both men and women in the workplace. In his official position, he stood out as an incorruptible manager.

Their courtship was characterized by having Bible studies together with prayers. They discussed their future and past together, but Mark never once mentioned the sexual abuse he had suffered, or the sexual fornication he had with the prostitutes when he was twice on an official assignment.

After marriage, Mark and Leah experienced a great honeymoon period, which virtually continued till the birth of their first child. Thereafter, Mark was a perfect example of a husband, doting over Leah. He went on several official assignments locally and internationally without any incident with any lady or temptation to yield to any desire to have sex with any prostitute again. However, he never shared with Leah all the succumbing he had to seasonal sexual desires in the past, and the women he had been involved with.

As a growing minister, Mark was mentored by senior ministers who, by their way of life, told him that he alone was necessary for the work of God. He was told that His wife is just to support so he must be able to keep things about his parishioners confidential without letting his wife know about it. Thus Mark thought it was okay for him to relate exclusively to women in and outside the church and keep their secrets, discussions, and problems only to himself without sharing this with his wife Leah. This was the inroad to having emotional affairs with other women who would call him at different times of the day; and, when he was on phone with them, he would walk away from his wife. As he poured himself into finding spiritual solutions for these women, he rarely shared the details with his wife.

Occasionally he would mention to Leah his wife, "Let's pray for Sister Cynthia because 'she is facing hard times.'" Even when he scheduled visits to these sisters, he went alone and the deceptive part of him told him nothing was wrong as long as he kept himself holy. Truly, in some cases Mark was really a "holy man of God" in some relationships, but he was drained emotionally. He never heard about emotional affairs, and he did not realize that he was giving out all the great part of his time and prayer life ministering to other people.

He also believed another fallacy that as long as you keep taking care of other people, God will take care of your own. Wrong! Wrong!! Wrong!!! Gradually, a widening gap came between this husband and wife and their coming together became a family business where they just discussed bills, the children, and school. At first, they had sex when they wanted, but it gradually came to the point where when Leah wanted sex, Mark had excuses of why he did not want it. However, when he wanted sex, he knew how to talk Leah into getting his own way and she would usually allow it to prevent him from sulking.

As the emotional vacuum between them became bigger, there were more irritations and arguments on issues, especially concerning Mark's involvement with his church activities. Mark found it more convenient to go straight from work to attend church activities, and when he did come home, it was just to sleep or do the office work he had brought home.

Mark was sent by his employers to a very senior management course. As all the professionals gathered together for the first day of class, the lust in Mark was at work again and his lustful eyes singled out a tall, loud lady in the class called Esther. Her manner of provocative dressing caused her to be attractive to Mark, and he started a conversation with her after class, and they began to look out for each other in classes. Soon Mark started dressing more to impress Esther, and when Leah noticed this and inquired as to what was going on, he merely remarked that he just wanted to be dressing well for the class. He did not mention that he had started lusting after another woman again and needed help.

From the conversation that Mark had with Esther, he had quickly identified a prayer burden which gave the emotional relationship a spiritual coloration. Esther had been married for some years without a child, and this was the deceptive spiritual assignment that

Mark put up as a front to explain away his lustful adventure with Esther. The emotional attachment became stronger during lunch breaks. They looked out for each other after work with the pretext of discussing the class assignments and team projects. They started calling each other after office hours and late in the night. Lustful expressions made their ways into their e-mails and texts to one another.

This issue became a full crisis in Mark's home one weekend afternoon. Mark and Leah had an argument over a domestic issue, and Mark openly told Leah that he was no longer in love with Leah. He stopped short of saying that he was now lustfully involved with Esther, and this had created a great emotional gap between both of them. Leah packed her bags and wanted to leave the matrimonial home, and Mark realized his folly and called a family friend to come and help him beg his wife Leah to stay.

It was this incident that brought out again the serial deceptive life Mark had been living. Yet, instead of seeking for help, he kept all the details to himself and moved on with life. However, as he was hiding his emotional affairs with Esther from Leah, Esther was stepping up the game. She visited Mark's office, presented Mark as a friend, and planned to have lunch together with him and a mutual friend on a convenient day. This never materialized because Mark and Leah decided to move to another city and it was this relocation that actually cut off the emotional affair between Esther and Mark.

In the new church Mark and Leah started attending, they were treated as leaders and somehow their new city made them closer and yet still far from each other. Mark continued to see the ministry work as a priority, regarding his home as secondary. This wrong placement of priorities made Mark continue to place other people above his home and marriage. The gap between Mark and Leah continued to increase as Mark regarded all his dealings, especially with sisters, as God's work. Mark had this concept of keeping secret the secrets of all those he counseled. This gave Mark the room to tell Leah only the things he wanted her to know, thus giving himself more room to be manipulative and perfect his self-deception.

Mark quickly became attached emotionally to Sister Deborah, who had a family that wanted to serve God. Her husband was never in church, but he allowed his wife to bring all the children to church. Again there was a bounding between Mark and Sister Deborah that resulted in them looking out for each other when the service was over and there was always a hug. When food was served in the church, Sister Deborah ensured that Mark got his own share as quickly as possible.

However, Mark continued to get entangled with different emotional affairs. He would counsel on the phone without regard to family time together, which was especially important since he should have been spending time with their growing children who were becoming teenagers. Mark's theory was that as you do the works of God, He will take care of you. So he made praying and counseling time for every other person, but did not for members of his own family. The relationship between him and his wife was more like business where they just came together to discuss the bills and house maintenance. Intimacy was replaced with casual discussions, and both appeared very busy.

Meanwhile, Mark was complaining to his close fellow ministers that the church was not growing and he decided that it was because his wife Leah was not cooperating with him to allow God to move in the ministry. This was basically because she did not support his relationship and closeness with the females. Meanwhile, Mark continued to task Leah about doing her best for the Lord and never really shared his past and current involvements with the women in his life.

Leah, on her own, had become quite concerned because, not only was the ministry was not growing, but the family itself was barely making ends meet. She continued to pray, and the Holy Spirit kept telling her to ask her husband to reveal those things he had been keeping away from her. Leah brought this up with him a couple of times, but he would treat it lightly and just share a little information about an event or a person that Leah had been curious about.

One night, however, Mark felt moved by the Holy Spirit to share about his past experience of sleeping with prostitutes several years ago, before they formally got married, but when they were already engaged. When sharing this, Mark treated it as a matter of information only and said he had settled it between God and himself long ago. Leah was shattered and very devastated. She told Mark to tell her everything about his life or otherwise she would leave the marriage.

It was only at this point that Mark began to realize that he was not the person he was supposed to be. How could his wife, whom he loved so much and believed that was God's perfect choice for him, want to leave the relationship? So, at this point, he for the first time, attempted to share with Leah the salient points in his life. However, Leah told him he had to tell her all about of his life

It was at this point that God told Leah that He had sent her into Mark's life as a woman on assignment to break the generational curse that had been upon Mark and his ancestral line so that it would not flow down to their own children. This was an assignment that Leah was never aware of. She thought she was just marrying a sweetheart without blemish. She had kept herself pure from childhood and Mark was the first and only man that she had really loved and given herself to. How could God keep such a thing away from her?

Her first logical conclusion was to quit the marriage. She felt bitter and betrayed, not just by Mark, but by God, too. Her world literally stopped. She shaved off her head and told her children that somebody quite close to her died. She grieved for days because she knew some of the atrocities that Mark had done.

At this stage, they both sought counsel from God and their God sent an Ananias. Remember when Saul of Tarsus was converted on the road to Damascus? God had already prepared a specific servant of HIS called Ananias to handle the follow-up process of Saul's conversion. Just like God told Saul specifically that a man called Ananias would come, and he also told Ananias that he had to go to Saul, so God told Leah whom specifically she should call. God had told a "mother in Israel," who had experienced such a great disappointment in her marriage, but kept on faithfully to God, that she should be praying for this family, even before Leah and Mark reached this point in their marriage. God had prepared her for such a time as this and she had the initial answers Leah needed.

It was this "mother in Israel" who arranged for an initial counseling and deliverance session for Mark. It was during and after the initial deliverance sessions that Mark realized that he has been living a deceptive double life. God told Leah that the healing of their marriage was to be based on 100 percent truth, and it took some time for Mark to come up with the truth about everything about his life. This was what was needed so that the work of grace could begin to be applied to restore him back to faith and gradually build him back up.

God sent further divine teachers and guides to Mark and Leah, but like He had told Leah, she was the one sent on assignment for Mark and she had to be led of God to perform another deliverance session on Mark which no other minister could have been strategically placed to perform. One morning, after praying together, as Leah was about to go to the bathroom, the Holy Spirit told her to turn back and ask her husband again if there were still some things untold. By this time, Mark felt convinced he should tell her everything that was outstanding. But as he made to speak, his voice ceased, and his body started to vibrate uncontrollably, and he could not talk.

Leah then started pleading the blood of Jesus. Leah followed the leading of the Holy Spirit, and then Mark confessed the incest between him and his stepsister, who was also born out of incest to his father. This started from childhood, as their grandmother laid them side by side, and that was the sexual entrance to the control of his life. When Mark's mother gave birth to him, she handed him over spiritually to the grandmother who then took control, and from that time, she put in him a sexual desire which started with the stepsister and was manifested in several other ways. That was the root entrance to his perverse sexual life.

Leah took authority, in the name of Jesus, and commanded the evil spirit to come out of Mark. A voice challenged Leah, saying that it was in control and had wrecked the Mark's golden years. Again, Leah took authority based on the marriage covenant between her and Mark and before God and man claimed the right to Mark: the controlling spirit did not have a right to him again. Mark was set free by the Holy Spirit.

For the first time, Mark, after this incident, now saw that the wrong choices he made all along his life were paths of destruction that would-perpetuate the generational curses that had been upon his family for another five generations. Mark just realized that, even though he had given his life to Christ, his secret, pleasurable sins were the gateway to limitations in his life, and that the lust of the eyes and flesh are pathways to complete self-destruction.

If the destruction had been only to Mark, one could say he deserved it. But it was after his deliverance that he saw the great damage his choices had done to Leah. His wrong, selfish, and wicked acts had brought untold hardships on Leah in so many areas of her life. His wrong choices had brought her shame and reproach among the women he had used to manifest his wicked deeds. He now realized that really there was no pleasure in sin, but only sorrow and shame. The countless nights that Leah could not sleep, or pull herself together were quite devastating for Mark.

He wished he had never done this. He saw that it was purely the mercy of God that he had not died in his sins, for he would have gone straight to hell. He saw that the fear of God, which is the beginning of wisdom, had eluded him when he was hiding his sins. He repented before God in prayers and fasting and subjected himself to further deliverance and counseling from minsters of God that God directed them to. He told Leah that, based on what he had done, he did not deserve to be in the relationship any longer. He had by his own wrong, selfish and wicked choices, sent himself out of the marriage: but God and Leah each chose to have mercy on him and gave him a second chance.

From then on, he realized 100 percent and nothing less is what he would practice with Leah for the rest of their lives together. No more secret sins would come between him and God. Now he knows that all sins will be uncovered, so it's better not to commit any than to plan to cover them. Mark realized he had trampled upon the innocent, precious, beautiful flowers in Leah that God had given him, and now he is hanging on tenaciously to the promise of God for restoration. No more separation emotionally, spiritually and physically exists between Mark and Leah.

They now review all their activities together as Mark now knows this is the only golden opportunity he has to actually fulfill his purpose in life as God and Leah have given him a second chance. Mark made a fresh vow and commitment to love and cherish Leah and to honor, respect and never take his eyes of Leah again while both of them shall live. Mark is daily haunted by the fact that he had shattered the dreams and desires of an innocent pure lady who given herself to him without any reservation. How can he repair a broken egg? However, the God who creates has promised Mark and Leah a new beginning. Mark resolved to court Leah all over again and trust God to mercifully continue His work of healings in Leah's life.

This awareness also made him realize that he had wrongly accused Leah of slowing down God's work, while all along; it was God's mercy and Leah's intercessory prayers that had sustained them. With the kind of double life he had lived, he should have been dead long ago. Mark now knows God is a Holy God and because of his second chance, he has to be about God's given assignment with His fear and walk in holiness. Mark can now identify with David as he turned around in Psalm 51 and resolved to work before God and flee all appearances of evil henceforth in his life. Sometimes Mark asks himself why God had not set him free earlier Why did any of the men and women of God he has met not tell him by discernment that he was living a double life?

However, the Bible says that the heart of man is so desperately wicked. Mark, by allowing the pleasure of little sins that were destroying him, did not think deeply enough to lay all on the altar to God. It was only when he decided to walk the path of truth with Leah that he realized he has literally limited his ability to appropriate the full blessings of God. Now Mark prays daily to God to search him and clean him of the assumptions and presumptions in his life that constitute sin. Now, he realizes that he needs a daily holy walk with the Lord and that he can allow no self-deception in himself again

For Leah, God has helped her to maintain her sanity. The heartbrokenness and betrayal she experienced almost took her life. Her health was challenged as a result of this awareness; she almost lost her job because she went through a lot of stress that the Holy Spirit helped her daily to overcome. She asked God why she did not know.

Yet she had been quite spiritual and in good standing with God all of those years. She can identify with Joseph, who had to go through all kinds of ordeals with betrayals and pains, until he got to Pharaoh's palace and became the prime minister. It was only then that the big picture of his suffering was made clear. He was to be the deliverer of Israel and the then world from famine. And like the brothers of Joseph who, at the initial confrontation with Joseph, still denied and kept to their lie of an animal killing their young brother, so also Mark initially kept his story of self-deception. However, God revealed his sins, as He did to David. Then Mark acknowledged his sins, repented of them, and promised Leah he would forever be faithful in all his life to God, and to the covenant and commitment between them.

The challenge is quite much for Leah. How can she forgive Mark? How can she ever trust Mark again? Details of all these will possibly be shared in another work, as the Holy Spirit directs, but the challenge here is for you to discover what your God given assignment is in your own relationships. Since this book is essentially about relationships, you must ask yourself this question and be clear in your understanding of your purpose and assignment in that relationship. Mark and Leah decided to keep their marriage intact and they are still working on it as the Author and Finisher of their faith, the Lord Jesus Christ, is helping them.

Woe unto them that seek deep to hide their counsel from the LORD,
and their works are in the dark, and they say,
Who seeth us? and who knoweth us? --Isaiah 29:15

Chapter 10

THE CHURCH, CHRISTIANS, AND MARKETPLACE

Somehow I initially felt not adequately prepared by the church to occupy the roles and expectations for my career as I climbed upwards. The church then had this maxim of not getting mixed up with the world. Yet we need to be successful managers in every assignment and give proper and fit leadership in all areas of life. This aspect of occupying effectively in the marketplace will be discussed further.

Missing Link between Church and Career in the Secular World

So, I found a great abyss between what the church teaches every Sunday and mid-week Bible Studies and Prayer meeting and the life many so called Christians live at their working places, business arenas, and social functions. Many Christians are living below God's expectation. Some Christians drink and get drunk. Some indeed do defraud their establishments and yet look prosperous in church through giving fat offerings, and tithes, and some generous donations.

Others have mistresses or woman friends with whom they have extra-marital affairs. Some fall into temptation when they are traveling out of working stations, attending seminars and conferences, going for further training from work places, and other opportunities that take them away from their home area where they are known to places where they have opportunities to enjoy their carnal and sinful cravings. Unfortunately, many do not see anything wrong in all these anti-Christian and unscriptural activities.

Seriously, I have to struggle with this and I found it difficult to correlate it with what I believe and with what the churches teach as doctrine and stand for on Sundays. I found myself not adequately equipped by the church or any Christian ministry I had ever been either in to deal with this issue. There are a great many discrepancies and differences between many Christians' life in the churches, at their homes, and in the secular arena. What can I do? Where can I now learn how to balance, handle, or cope with these great and unspeakable differences I see in the conduct, conversation, and commitment of some who claim to be Christian?

Clearly, the market place and the church are quite different. The market place is controlled by mindset of secularism, humanism, and commercialism. There are social activities that seem normal in the marketplace but are anti-Bible and anti-God. The lifestyles and social culture of the market place are, most of the time, incompatible with that of the Bible. The quest, the approach to life and money matters, the relationship and dealings may look neat, but underneath there are filths indescribable. This is the same market place where both Christians and non-Christians seek employment for living. This is the same arena we all work and to achieve something in life. For Christians, the struggle begins when they get to know what the real meaning of the words, "world and worldliness."

In my opinion, based on my perspective and experience, many Christian churches and ministries do not truly prepare Christian believers to be able to face the market place and still maintain their faith, commitment, and consecration to God. This is one of the reasons for double standards of life, carnality, and worldliness we see when we witness defeated Christian living in the market places in our world.

Definitions of the Marketplace

What is the marketplace? The marketplace is simply an area in a town where a public mercantile establishment is set up. The term *market* describes the world of commercial activity where goods and services are bought and sold. In strict technical terms, competition is the order in market and market place; without competition, there would be no market; competition is the driving force of the marketplace. This is where both Christians and non-Christians converge to demonstrate their skills, expertise, knowledge, and gifts, potential and so on. So, it turns out that in all ramifications, competition is the axiom and *sine qua non* that the Christians will face. This is very different from the Church setting. Do you agree with me?

In addition, a marketplace is the space, actual or metaphorical, in which a market operates. The term is also used in a trademark law context to denote the actual consumer environment, i.e. the "real world" in which products and services are provided and consumed. The question in this consumerist environment is, how can a Christian live, work, cope, and move ahead without becoming a consumerist? Friends, are Christians prepared adequately to cope or handle this consumerist behavior? I bet many of us become consumerists in the market place and become "saints" in church or Christian environment. We have a more complex problem because most establishments are owned by the non-Christians and Christians are at their mercy.

My Researches and Findings of This Matter

Having exposure and experience in the marketplace as I pursued my life's career left me in a quest to fill this vacuum of inadequate preparation that many Christians face in the marketplace challenges. I must admit that I was confronted with many temptations and trials: With God's help, I was victorious. I then came to the conclusion that the church of God needs to revisit the need for discipleship so that it can help human, spiritual, and social development in light of the Bible. We need to get Christian believers ready to live, work, and accomplish God's purpose in the world without joining or loving the world. Later in life, I had opportunity to further my study in Theology and I took it upon myself to research more on this matter. The topic of my research was "CHRISTIAN LEADERSHIP…WHY CHRISTIAN LEADERS FAIL IN THE CORPORATE WORLD."

In my thesis I hypothesized: Are Christian's leaders adequately prepared to face the challenges in the marketplace? If they are well prepared, why do they fail? What is the significant value of their success or failure?

To carry out this research and hypothesis, I set out to ask others to answer my questionnaire. The questionnaire was administered to people with the purpose to find out criteria for measuring successful Christian leaders in the marketplace. The research was on leadership in the church and their roles in understanding, communicating, and helping believers realize the purpose of God in relation to success in the things of God as well as in the secular world of business, economy, politics, etc.

The Values That Make a Leader

The Competency Approach of leadership teaches us that leadership should have the following characteristics:

- Multi-skill - Required to undertake any challenge, be it spiritual or secular

- Resilience – Ability to stand the test of time, unwavering

- Wisdom and knowledge – Required for balance, creativity / innovation, and change management

- Financial management – Financial literacy and prudence

- Servant leadership – Demonstrating leadership through service and personal example

- Sexual control – A disciplined avoidance of sexual misconduct

- Marital sanctity – Maintaining a home that is peaceful and godly

Results and Analysis from the Questionnaire

1. *The successful Christian leader is seen as a servant leader in every true sense and not just the "Number 1."*

Servant Leadership

Servant leadership is at the heart of Christian leadership. Servant leadership is different from servant hood. All Christians, not just leaders, are called to be servants, serving each other, following Jesus' example in washing His disciples' feet, and loving our neighbors as ourselves. Along with that call to servant hood is the need we each have to allow ourselves to receive from Jesus, just as He washed His disciples' feet. When Peter protested, Jesus told him, *"Unless I wash you, you have no part with me"* (John 13:8).

What underpins servant leadership is the motivation behind our actions as leaders. If personal desire were the sole decision criterion, Jesus would have chosen not to go through the pain and suffering on the cross. In the Garden of Gethsemane, Jesus prayed, *"Father, if you are willing take this cup from me, yet not my will, but yours, be done"* (Luke 22:42). The weight of the burden of taking not only our guilt but also our sins had become too heavy. Even at this point, Jesus could have gotten up and walked away. However, Jesus modeled servant leadership throughout His ministry. This will require us also to set aside personal gain, to make sacrifices, and to put the needs of others above the direction we may prefer for ourselves. You've probably met people who are highly career minded, people whose main motivation is to get in a position where they will gain some reward. This is what happens in many marketplaces. This is the complete opposite of the leadership Jesus demonstrated.

Some may suggest that servant leaders are weak. However, nothing could be further from the truth. They model integrity where their thoughts, words, and actions flow from a consistent desire. The word integrity comes from the Latin word meaning whole or complete, as in integer, or whole number. One of the biggest reasons leaders lose the respect of their followers is that they lack true integrity where their private lives and thoughts do not match their public statements, or where they are inconsistent, adopting principles that are popular and appropriate to the moment rather than sticking to their underlying, but potentially unpopular, principles. Maintaining integrity is not always easy!

Servant leadership is not a particular style of leadership but rather relates to the motivation behind a leader's thoughts, words, and actions. Leaders can fit any of the six leadership styles described by our leadership style indicator and still be very much a servant leader. Servant leaders are not leaders on the basis of their position or leadership role, but rather lead according to their calling, vision, and principles. One of the challenges for servant leaders is to ensure that their vision and principles are in line with others in their organization; and, therefore, it is highly important for them to engage with others to develop a common vision and shared values.

Whilst serving others as the heart of leadership may not appear easy, it is perhaps in one sense easier for a leader to be consistent with the vision and values they hold for themselves rather than always seek to live up to the vision of others. The latter requires constantly trying to create an image, seeking opportunities to sell themselves, or trying to read the political signals sent out by others.

2. *The successful Christian leader must show a track record (testimony) of grace in the area of sexual conduct by avoiding every form of sexual immorality.*

The Bible says, *"Keep on running away from sexual immorality. Any other sin that a person commits is outside his body, but the person who sins sexually sins against his own body. You know that your body is a sanctuary of the Holy Spirit who is in you, whom you have received from God, don't you? You do not belong to yourselves, because you were bought for a price. Therefore, glorify God with your bodies."* (1 Corinthians 6:18-20, ISV).

Someone has rightly observed the influence of Christianity in the world at large, saying that Christianity affects, with its leaven-like virtue, the whole civil and social life of a people and leads it on the path of progress in all genuine civilization; that it nowhere prescribes a particular form of government and carefully abstains from all improper interference with political and secular affairs; that it accommodates itself to monarchical and republican institutions; and that it can flourish even under oppression and persecution from the State, as the history of the first three centuries sufficiently shows. However, it teaches the true nature and aim of all government and the duties of rulers and subjects; it promotes the abolition of bad laws and institutions and the establishment of good; it is in principle opposed alike to despotism and anarchy; it tends, under every form of government, towards order, propriety, justice, humanity, and peace; and it fills the ruler with a sense of responsibility to the supreme king and judge, and the ruled with the spirit of loyalty, virtue, and piety.

Giving Our Teens and Youth a Proper Understanding of Sex

As we peep back through history, looking through our land and all civilized lands, one of the most conspicuous facts concerning the power of sex is its frightful destructiveness. The spectacle of wasted manhood and womanhood, of depleted powers in body, mind, and soul, is present in history and is even more appalling in contemporary society. It is so oppressive that it has driven many thoughtful men and women to despair. Men and women, otherwise hopeful and purposeful, here become gloomy and fatalistic; they have no hope that their lust will ever be effectively controlled.

Such pessimism, however, contradicts the history as well as the instincts of the race. In the face of great evils, there have always been those who would sit down in discouragement and despair; every great destructive force in human history has daunted some men to the point of inactivity. Yet the evils have been controlled. Ignorant and fearful people have said, "This thing is beyond human power; it is useless for us to struggle against fate." Yet men of vision and of courage have struggled and won. No man of moral passion and religious purpose can adopt an attitude of passive submission to the forces of destruction. We can admit no necessary evil or the battle of human progress is lost.

We ask ourselves soberly, therefore, how this tremendous outrush of destructive energy may be controlled. The answer is plain. Human beings have by the agency of fire itself constructed the means by which fire is controlled and domesticated; they have turned disease against itself, and by the agency of antitoxins have conquered it; they are learning to arouse and organize the fighting spirit of man against his own most ancient and fearful expression and are enlisting soldiers of peace in a war against war. Even so the race depends upon the higher affections for control of the lower, and lust is controlled by love.

I talked once to a young man in college who had given himself over to sexual vice when he was in high school; until a year before I spoke with him, he had supposed that virtually all men were and must be sexually indulgent. For twelve months he had kept himself clean. I inquired why and how. He replied simply that he had fallen in love with a young woman and wished to marry her. His former course now seemed to him shameful and unmanly. Lust yielding to love!

In one of his sonnets to the woman who afterward became his wife, Edmund Spenser writes, "You frame my thoughts and fashion me within: You stop my tongue and teach my heart to speak: You calm the storm that passion did begin: Strong through your cause, but by your virtue weak."[4] In our own experience, as far as we have achieved victory in our own bodies and minds over our baser passions, we have achieved it by the power of the higher

---

[4] Edmund Spenser

affections. It is a fact of common experience that love calms the storm that passion did begin. So Spenser's lady strengthened passion by her charm, but weakened it by her virtue.

Nor is this the only higher affection that, in the practical experience of men, has controlled and transformed animal passion. Thousands of fully sexed men have through the centuries turned their bodily and mental energies so fully to devoted service for God and their fellows as to rise above the clamoring demands of physical appetite, in the vigorous terms of the New Testament, making themselves eunuchs for the kingdom of God's sake. This is a hard saying, and the experience it brings must always be confined to a small number of men; yet it goes far toward demonstrating a general possibility, and it should effectively dispose of the "necessity" argument by which men often excuse their vicious practices.

One thing more should be said on this subject of control. Not only are the higher, more spiritual affections the most effective masters of the lower, they are the only effective masters. Public reprobation can do much, but it is ineffectual with large numbers of relatively unattached members of society, and it is impotent against secret vice. Motives of cautious fear are always weak with full-blooded and generous youth, and they are likely to become weaker with all men as medical science discovers ways to prevent or escape the most obviously fearful consequences of sexual license.

A familiar phrase comes to my mind, as no doubt it comes to yours: "The expulsive power of the higher affections"; yet I think that phrase is not quite suitable. It is not a question of expulsion: It is not wholly a question of control: it is mainly a question of direction. What we need today with boys and girls for the solving of the sex problems is to direct those energies, which in their false direction are destructive, into right and healthful ways; that is, we need to socialize and elevate that affection which in baser forms has aspects of ugly animalism.

As one solution to the problem of control it has been proposed to separate the sexes in the adolescent years. From my point of view, this would defeat our object. In the association of boys and girls during the adolescent period, we may enlist the higher affections for the control and direction of the powers that are set free by sexual impulses developed in that very period of life.

What happens in the experience of the normal boy? In this period of early adolescence he finds within himself a wonderful quickening of mind, impulses, feelings, and longings that he does not understand. These impulses, feelings, and longings perplex him, possibly for years. They reach out vaguely and blindly toward the opposite sex, sometimes in a perverted way, but more often naturally and honestly. Then the young man falls in love. At once his more or less vague, cloudy, incoherent, formless feelings and purposes are concentrated, directed, and fixed in devotion to a young woman whom he idealizes, almost deifies. That is the first stage in the natural directing and forming of sexual powers and impulses toward social, moral, and religious ends.

Of course the young man may discover after a while that the first object of his fancy is not as angelic as he thought. By and by, his fancy changes and may rove to several other maidens before he reaches maturity; but each successive experience, if he is true to his better self, concentrates his affections and directs them until, if he is fortunate, in the course of time he finds his true mate and enters upon marriage. He is now fairly equipped for what most of us know to be a long course in the discipline of the selfish, the personal, the more or less brute desires and ambitions of man.

Here he learns to subject himself, his own comfort, his own ends, his own ambitions, to the good of his wife and her happiness, to the good of his children and the satisfaction of their needs. Then, more and more, after having concentrated the powers of his spirit through faithful courtship, happy marriage, and fatherhood, the man is able to diffuse these same energies through many channels for the protection of all sorts and conditions of women and children. The man is now a citizen, a member of society, with developed powers of social sympathy, of social energy.

How has he developed these powers? Not by any supposition that the early sex instincts he felt in his boyhood were wholly animal and must be atrophied by disuse, but by gathering and directing them into the right channels. Direction, like control, depends upon enlightened, purposeful, persistent love.

The Matter of Sex, Flesh, and the Soul

In the next place, we may consider how, in matters of sex, the flesh and the soul may grow together in mutual help. The essential facts and the vital importance of the sex life appeal to the developing boy or girl in four great relations: in relation to father and mother, in relation to the strength and grace of his or her own body and mind, in relation to his or her future family, and in relation to society in general. These appeals come in successive periods and open the way to healthful instruction and guidance from childhood up to manhood and womanhood.

Sex questions first arise in the child's mind in connection with parenthood. The first thing a little boy or girl needs to know is that the young life is sheltered and fed during long months in the mother's body, and that the father had a share in that life. Is it not amazing that, in this twenty-first century, we find many girls twelve years old and over who do not know their father had any biological input or contribution in starting their lives? I knew of a girl nineteen years old, a student in college, who did not know that a man had any essential involvement in bringing children into the world, but supposed, when any question of illegitimate childbirth was raised, that possibly God punished a bad woman by sending her a baby before she was married. It is little short of criminal that many girls are allowed to reach adolescence with no knowledge of sex except such as they have received directly or indirectly from animals.

If boys and girls knew from the beginning that a part of the father's life and a part of the mother's life united to form the beginning of their lives, the question of sex would begin on a plane where there were religious, moral, and spiritual associations, and an atmosphere of love and holiness. These young people could then see the facts of sex clearly instead of through the mists of prurient fancy and suggestion as they see them now. The boy and girl, who know these two tremendous facts, of the nurturing care of the mother before birth and the cooperation of the father and mother in the beginning of life, are fortified against the principal moral and spiritual dangers that they are to face in the future.

The next information and guidance needed by our boys and girls concerns the influence of sex upon their own development. The objection is continually raised that it is not well for little children to have sexual thoughts emphasized in their minds. But, at present, no boy or girl grows up and plays among other children, or hears talk on the streets, or goes to work in factory or store, without hearing these facts emphasized day by day—emphasized unhealthily and distorted shamefully. We propose simply to have the emphasis shifted and lightened. It will be lightened as the facts are given truly and in right relations, essentially by parents.

Boys and girls should learn, at the same time they are learning facts of nutrition, excretion, respiration, and circulation of the blood, those facts regarding sex which are most important for healthy growth of mind and body. They should know that the organs of reproduction have a definite relation to the natural and healthful development of the full powers of their bodies in future years. They should understand that internal secretions of these organs coming into the blood help to build up bones and muscles, help to make their nerve fibers active and vigorous, help to form their brains, and help to equip them for manly strength and womanly grace in the years to come. These are very simple matters. These facts of sex can be conveyed by just a few sentences of clear, considerate, wise information at the right time, in relation to the other facts of bodily development.

Understanding Puberty, Sex, and Socialization

Considering now the period of puberty, we find additional needs, for no boy or girl reaches puberty, under ordinary conditions, without knowing that it brings the possibility of fatherhood and motherhood: that it brings the possibility of process we call fertilization, in which the life of plants and animals begins. The boy or girl who reaches this age has a right to know what fertilization means and what fertilization implies; has a right to the simple biological facts which will tell him the relation between the life of the parents and the life of the child, the mysterious relation in body and mind that we call heredity.

The beginning of the socializing of sex energy and sex power depends upon recognition of the fact that this power that develops in the young man and young woman at puberty is not to be used for selfish gratification, it is not primarily a source of pleasure, but has a very direct relation to the health, intelligence, and happiness of others. This relation may be enforced by a simple study of succeeding generations of flowers and the ways in which forms, colors, and sizes originate and are handed down from generation to generation in wonderful variety. Or it may be illustrated from an observation of the beginnings of sex in infusoria, how tiny animals in stagnant water grow to full size and each divides simply into two to form a new generation; how this simple asexual process continuing for several generations results in growing weakness and old age, steadily decreasing size, steadily decreasing vitality, until there comes a time when one infusion unites with another. There is where sex begins. That union of two individuals is required to restore youth, to refresh vitality and energy, and to produce greater variety in the forms of life. When a boy or girl knows these simple facts, they are better able to understand the power of reproduction than they possibly can if these facts are not presented to them, or if all they have heard has been ceaseless reiteration of the pleasures of selfish indulgence of sexual appetite.

Finally, when the boy and girl come into later adolescence and face manhood and womanhood, they are ready to know some of the larger social aspects of sex. They are ready to know of the diseases brought on by perverted sex habits; of the frightful waste of those who give themselves to licentiousness: of the frightful waste of strength and youthful energy not only in those who actually die, but in those that survive. More than that, seeking right relations of them to society, they need to know the social aspects of sex. The young man needs to know what it means for a woman to bear a child; he needs to know the social and economic dependence of the pregnant woman and the young mother so that he may realize what the power of fatherhood means in the actual work of society.

I cannot imagine any man talking glibly of the necessary evil, of man's inability to control sex passions, if he truly understands the social facts of sex. Any young man who knows even a part of the burden his mother bore for him, if he has a spark of manhood in his being, is surely fortified against temptation to such selfish indulgence. If, beyond that, he can see the relationship of the home to society, the relative steadiness and dependability of a worker with a wife and children, who bears the home burdens in a man's way, as compared with the floating, homeless wanderer who walks our streets; if he knows these central facts and the dependence of the home upon the faithfulness of the man and the presence of the man; if he has a spark of patriotism in his heart, then he must realize the necessity for the socialization of that passion which, though it began in individual and selfish forms, issues in such fateful social consequences.

The solution of this great, urgent problem, which we feel the weight of more and more in these years of careful investigation of our social conditions, will come in frankly recognizing the beginnings upon which the whole sex life in mind and body is based, and in transforming fundamentally important animal instincts and desires into higher affections and in humanizing them for the sake of the loved one, for the sake of family, and for the sake of the social brotherhood and sisterhood in which we are members.

Sacredness and Consecration of Sex

My closing word in this part is one which seems to me most significant of the true, the beautiful, the victorious way out of so much discouragement and so much crime. That is, the word *consecration*. That word includes two essential ideas: the ideas of sacredness and cooperation. The problems of sex will never be solved until the sacredness of sex is recognized, for sex is vitally and indissolubly bound up with the two greatest facts that you and I know. The greatest fact of the organized world around us is life, the greatest fact of the spiritual world into which we lift our souls is love: The beginnings of both life and love are in sex. No boy or girl will readily understand what life means except as they have some clear, wise teaching about sex; no boy or girl will fully understand what love means except through recognition of the dignity and worth and purity of the fundamental facts and powers of sex.

Who shall give this enlightenment? I think it must be clear that this enlightenment cannot be given by the very young and inexperienced person, but that the facts can be rightly given only by some person who knows the sacredness of this relationship for himself or herself. They can best be given by a mature person who has seen and felt what they mean. In the long run, I have no doubt that our boys and girls will get the information they must have from their parents, for the father and the mother are the best qualified to give it. I have named both the father and the mother, for the solution of our problem does not only in knowing the sacredness of sex, it is also in working together for the elevation of the sex life. We men shall not be able, in the future, to sit down and say, "Oh, well, John will learn from his mother" or "Mary's mother will make that clear to her" or "Their mother does these things." It will not be possible for the socializing of the sex instincts and the ripening of the sex powers to be made clear to young people except as men and women both recognize the sacredness of the sexual relation and undertake to make things clear to boys and girls.

Men must give up their selfish indifference to evil conditions, and women—some women—must give up the bitterness and hardness that come into their hearts and their faces when they think of the suffering their gender has endured at the hands of men. This is not a problem for one gender alone: It cannot be solved by either half of the great whole of humanity. We know this to be true in our personal life; it is equally true in our social life. It is only by the girding-up of the whole spirit of the man to go forth and meet his duty as a lover, as a husband, as a father, and it is only by the girding-up of all the powers of the woman to lead and to help, that the family can be organized. In this great human family of ours, the man and the woman in days that are coming will cooperate to remove from our midst the blackest and most fearful perversion of the natural powers of our race.

We do not believe in sitting down idly before this problem and saying, "It has always been, it always will be." In this great day of moral and spiritual progress, with powers that we have inherited from our forefathers in this land and other lands, we know that there is no necessary evil. We are learning what the evil of sex is, and how it arises, and we are beginning to use the forces at hand for its destruction. Conscience is kindling and determination is hardening among our people that this thing shall cease to be. The ape and the tiger shall yet die from our midst, and man's spirit shall triumph in his flesh.[5]

Apostle Paul gives this admonition, in 1 Thessalonians 5:22—"*Abstain from every form of evil.*" The word "form" here is something that strikes the eye, or which is out in the open. It is the external appearance or shape of something. Our passage probably carries the idea of "sort, kind." There are many kinds of evil out there — including doctrinal error. The word "abstain" means "to hold oneself from" (4:3). Invariably, this word refers to evil practices whether doctrinal or moral (Acts 15:20, 29; 1 Timothy 4:3; 1 Peter 2:11). Christians are to keep themselves from foul doctrine. We should not play with evil teaching. We should distance ourselves from it. The phrase "form of evil" is a contrast to the phrase in verse 20, "*hold fast what is good.*" Christians are to avoid anything that smacks of bogus doctrine. They cannot do this if they have not examined the Word of God thoroughly. Hold yourselves aloof from any prophecy that is not based in truth from the Bible. *"Every form of evil"* does not restrict itself to those things that appear evil. Rather, we must recognize that evil, including false doctrine, may manifest itself in any visible outward form. However, when evil clearly manifests itself, believers must keep their distance lest they be implicated in it. (Num. 16:26).

3. *The successful Christian leader must show strength in the face of adversity.*

For some adversity is a daily companion. For others, it is an occasional reality. As believers, we also will face adversity and therefore we need to give some serious thought to whether we are relating to it in a healthy, biblical way or not. Doing so will open our eyes to how much of God's Word addresses the issue of adversity. This is an important theme throughout the entire Bible.

Adversity, Christians, and the Bible

Adversity is the necessary consequence of sin's entrance into the world, and it affects believers and unbelievers alike. Everyone will face adversity, which may or may not be

---

[5] A. Forel, The Sexual Question, chap. XII, "Religion and Sexual Life"; William James, Varieties of Religious Experience, chap. I;

related to our choices or actions, in which God or the devil may be involved. Learning to handle adversity well will result in purification of our motives, strengthening of our faith in God's deliverance, and freedom from the bondage of needing to be comfortable, among other things. This is the biblical perspective.

In a great number of North American Evangelical homes today, Elisabeth Elliot is a household word. Her radio program, "Gateway to Joy," is broadcast on some 250 English-speaking stations and 250 more in translation. She speaks of "soldierly qualities" and the need for a cross-bearing Christianity. She reiterates the need for wives to be submissive to husbands. She challenges outright the dating practices of our youth. Simply put, she advocates for a Christianity that is a striking contrast to much of what fills the "bestseller" section in Christian bookstores today.

But Elisabeth Elliot may be best-known as the surviving wife of Jim Elliot, the twenty-eight-year-old missionary speared to death in 1956 with four of his co-laborers: Nate Saint, Pete Fleming, Roger Youderian, and Edward McCully. Along with their wives and children, these five men were involved in the early efforts of reaching the Auca tribe (now known as the Huaorani) in the dense jungles of northern Ecuador. They were nervous but optimistic as they landed their small Piper aircraft on a shallow part of the Curaray River. Elliot's riveting account of this story and the follow-up to it, *Through Gates of Splendor* and *The Savage, My Kinsman*, quickly became standard missionary fare and remains so today, over fifty years later. The event itself—known as the Palm Beach incident for the shallow beach where the plane landed—continues to have a riveting impact on successive generations of young people. Countless youth have been called to service in the fields of harvest as a result. All have been called to live lives of increasing sanctification.

As a prolific writer of over twenty books who has moved well beyond the pale of mission-focused material, Elliot has focused her writing efforts across the last two decades to a range of topics, including God's plan for the Christian family, suffering, loneliness, and a re-evaluation of Christian dating. While some find her a bit harsh and dogmatic, she has articulated a spiritual passion in the face of all of life's hardships that has given many a more upright spiritual posture.

Elliot's immediate response to the Palm Beach incident placed her, along with co-laborer Rachel Saint (sister of the slain Nate Saint), in the memory of Evangelicals as modern-day saints. Shortly after the incident, she returned to the tribe to continue the church-planting work among the Huaorani. They made it clear they did not want to prosecute the murderers. Today, the numerous Huaorani followers of Wnagogi ("creator God") may well be her most profound legacy. The sweet, though costly irony, was illustrated most poignantly as Stephen Saint, son of martyred Nate Saint, was baptized by a Huaorani pastor—one of the spear-wielding Indians who took part in the slaying of his father years earlier.

The living testimony of Elisabeth Elliot and Rachel Saint's work amongst the Huaorani is a superb example of the vital and strategic role of women in the frontier mission task. In addressing her preparedness for the initial tragedy, Elliot attributes her strength in adversity to her upbringing—one that had missions at its very core. Elliot wrote; "I grew up in a very strong, missionary-minded home. We had dozens, perhaps hundreds of missionaries visiting in our home. I have my mother's guest book that has 42 countries represented in it. Therefore, I had read missionary books, we had looked at thousands of missionary slides, heard many missionary stories and we knew that there would be hardships. Of course, I didn't know what the nature of mine might be and I didn't expect it to be quite so soon."[6]

She noted that in each of the major blows to her faith that first year in Ecuador, it was a return to the cross of Christ that provided the deepest counsel. But she recognizes that precious few have a similar background and its component part—preparedness for adversity—with which she was so blessed. "So, when I have the opportunity to speak to prospective missionaries, I do want to emphasize an encounter with the cross. I think it takes a deep, spiritual encounter with the cross before we're really qualified to call ourselves missionaries…" Elliot wrote.

While hesitant to generalize too broadly, Elliot sees in the younger generation an aversion, not so much to the grand cause of martyrdom, but to the mundane discipline of yielding to Christ's lordship in the small things. Her words to prospective cross-cultural workers: "I would take them first to the foot of the cross and just ask them if they understand what the cross was all about and what it means in our daily life. If Jesus told us that we must take up our cross daily and follow Him, in what tiny little ways might we experience this?"

"These students do know that five missionaries were killed in 1956 and that was a very dramatic event that is still in the minds of many," she continues. "I am amazed at how many decades have gone by and it seems as though more people are acquainted with that story now than when it happened. But the great question is the tiny, little things which are not dramatic and not heroic, but those are the ways the cross is going to be presented to us. I often ask a group, 'In what ways do you expect the cross to be presented to you?' Well, the chances are not very great that it is going to be anything dramatic or heroic; it is probably going to be, as John H. Newman put it, 'the carrying on of small duties which are distasteful to us.' My impression is that they have not had the same kind of earnestness and preparation for suffering. America loves comfort and fun. And we need to face squarely the words that 'If we endure, we shall also reign with Him' (2 Tim. 2:12)."12[7]

---

[6] From the work of Elisabeth Elliot

[7] Elisabeth Elliot

4. ***The successful Christian leader must display wisdom more than knowledge in certain situations.***

"The High Values"

Psychologists Christopher Peterson and Martin Seligman have identified specific character strengths and virtues. They include:

- *Wisdom and knowledge* – It's not just how much you know that counts, but how well you apply your knowledge to a beneficial purpose.

- *Creativity* – Leaders must innovate, and to do so they have to be willing to think and perceive in new ways and risk breaking out of stodgy old patterns.

- *Curiosity* – Leaders are open to new approaches and love to investigate and explore the unknown.

- *Open-mindedness* – They exercise critical thinking and don't jump to conclusions.

- *Love of learning* – They continually challenge themselves to learn new things and they enjoy doing it.

- *Perspective* – They are willing to examine a situation from several different points of view. They look for clarity.

- *Courage* – This is really an ability to marshal emotional strength despite opposing forces from others and within you.
- *Persistence* – People of character strive toward their goals in spite of setbacks.
- *Humanity* – Great leaders display love, kindness, and social intelligence.
- *Justice* – You want to be viewed as fair. Part of being fair is showing an appreciation for teamwork and loyalty. Don't underestimate the importance of being a good citizen. Other important values include extending mercy, having a sense of humor, and inspiring hope in others. As Napoleon once observed, "Leaders are dealers in hope."

A mentor is commonly defined as a wise and trusted counselor and teacher. The word mentor comes to us from the classical tradition. It is originally the name of a character in *The Odyssey*, an old and trusted friend of Odysseus who is left behind as the warriors embark for Troy to keep an eye on Odysseus' household. Odysseus' return is long delayed by many adventures and trials, and all is not well at home. His household is invaded by would-be suitors for Penelope, his longsuffering and faithful wife. Odysseus' son, Telemakhos, is increasingly incensed by the disrespect shown his parents, but uncertain of what to do. At this point, Mentor plays his important role as a wise counselor to the headstrong, wavering young man. He counsels continuing confidence in Odysseus' return and a mission to search for him. Mentor, the old and trusted friend of the father, links the wisdom and power of the past to the uncertainties of the future.

In *The Odyssey*, Mentor's role is actually played by Athena, the goddess of wisdom, disguising herself as Mentor. The goddess provides Telemakhos with the vision, resources, companionship, and encouragement he needs to act well in an unknown and threatening situation. The wisdom given to the young man is not only the hard-won knowledge gained through a long and fruitful life, it is also divine insight.[8] Mentoring is such a rich role because it shares a depth of caring and insight that builds a bridge to the future. In the words of "a wise and trusted counselor and teacher," one often can hear divine insight and derive the courage and faithfulness to act for what is best.

This poignant tale from classical antiquity, even as it affords insight into what mentoring is, also raises further questions. Every word in our brief definition, "wise," "trusted," "counselor," "teacher," can be understood in a variety of ways. Even the word "and" implies that the term combines qualities and roles and has more than a bit of ambiguity.

5. ***The successful Christian leader must have a good home as defined by the Bible (based on marriage between man and woman).***

A tremendous bastion of strength for orthodox laypeople in our circumstances is marriage and family life, a state that has been blessed by God for the salvation of each individual member of the family. In order fully to understand this, we must look at the doctrinal foundations of marriage found in Scripture and sacred traditions which are the ongoing conscience of the church.

The Bible's Views of Marriage

When we look at the practice of marriage, family life, and multiplication of the human race as described in the Old Testament, we are immediately aware that great emphasis was placed on the continuation of the Hebrew race. Endless family trees are given to us in the Old Testament. With the coming of Christ, marriage no longer had as its primary goal the reproduction of human beings and the perpetuation of a family line, although procreation was still regarded as an important part of marriage. But Christ had come to the world and brought with Him the proof and guarantee of the resurrection of the dead, therefore giving to Christian marriage a new primary goal—the attainment of eternal life by husband, wife, and all children.

The marriage service in the Orthodox Church begins with the words, "Blessed is the Kingdom, of the Father and of the Son and of the Holy Spirit, now and ever and unto the ages of ages. Amen." This exclamation emphasizes the seriousness of marriage and also the goal of marriage. According to the Church canons, those Orthodox Christians who

---

[8] This story is from the classical tradition about mentorship. It is originally the name of a character in *The Odyssey* and refers to an old and trusted friend of Odysseus.

marry outside the Church are deprived of the sacraments of the Church. Some people find this shocking: they feel the Church is being too harsh. But the question is: What gives validity to marriage? From a spiritual standpoint, what gives meaning to a marriage?

Unlike the wedding ceremonies in most non-Orthodox churches, marriage in the Orthodox Church is not a contract—a legal agreement with the exchange of vows or promises—between two people. Rather, marriage is the setting up, by two people, of a miniature church, a family church, wherein people may worship the true God and struggle to save their souls. It is also a family church that is in obedience to Christ's church. As Saint Basil the Great says, it is natural to marry, but it must be more than natural; it must be a yoke borne by two people under the Church. Thus we see that in New Testament times, the focus of marriage was switched from a primary purpose of producing children to a primary purpose of providing a way for human beings to save their souls. The wedding ceremony itself is filled with rich symbolism that makes this whole aspect of marriage very clear.

Demands on the leader are very exacting today. In a recent conference on leadership, the question "What makes a great leader?" was asked. The following list appeared:

- The leader must be wise.
- The leader must love people.
- The leader much be an effective change agent.
- The leader must manage people.
- The leader must be a visionary.
- The leader must have good interpersonal skills.
- The leader must be an effective coach.
- The leader must be a good husband.
- The leader must have a good family.

Christian writer Philip Yancey wrote that we push our pastors to function as psychotherapists, orators, priests, and chief executive officers. Meanwhile we place on them a unique burden of isolation and loneliness. Not only are they expected to perform a multiplicity of roles, the pressure to succeed is also incredibly great, especially when members compare them to pastors of mega-churches. We expect them to do everything well, and we want success to come quickly. Indeed, being a ministry leader is certainly one of the most difficult vocations today.

6. *The successful Christian leader must show a track record (testimony) of grace over the use of power (authority).*

A Christian Properly Uses His God- or Man-given Authority

Authority is legal power to force (people) to obey. *"Joseph was thirty years old when he entered the service of Pharaoh King of Egypt"* (Gen. 39:46). Joseph knew who gave him the authority as a leader. His own leader above him gave him the power. Every leader has a leader. Those who follow him/her place the authority on him/her. A person is not a leader when no one is following him or her. Joseph knew above all else his power as a leader came from God. A favorite Bible verse for church leaders is Acts 1:8*: "But you will receive power when the Holy Spirit comes on you. Then you will be my witnesses . . ."* (NIRV). Church leaders must understand that their leadership power comes from God. They also must understand that those they serve give them authority as leaders.

Church leaders use these blessings for the building up of the group or church. Their position as leaders is to succeed in carrying out God's purpose. Some leaders put their authority to an improper use, but those who do will suffer the results of putting their power to an improper use. A wise Christian leader does not forget that his leadership depends on the responsibility that goes with authority (2 Cor. 5:9-10). Responsibility is being able to think and act in a reasonable way.

Anyone capable of generating enthusiasm in others for the sake of an ideal or a cause is a leader. However, leadership comes in many guises and can be as diverse as Cesar Chavez or Mussolini. The history of philosophy provides numerous theories regarding leadership, organization, and motivation, some which appeal to base instincts and fear, and some which appeal to nobility and humanity.

Strictly pragmatic leadership manuals like Machiavelli's *The Prince* or Sun-Tzu's *The Art of War* are typical examples of philosophies that are more concerned with the exertion of power rather than true leadership. Using the simple lust for control as a guideline, the good leader here might be defined as one who maintains control over a populace, wages war effectively, instills fear in one's subjects, and holds on to power with tenacity. Other works on leadership, such as Plato's *Republic,* assert that leadership comes through a pursuit of wisdom and the understanding that the goal of a good citizen ought to be the acquisition of wisdom.

Lastly, counterfeit Christian leaders frequently abuse their authority over their followers. Peter may allude to this in Peter 2:10 ("despise authority . . . self-willed") and 2:18 ("speaking out arrogant words of vanity"). They usually do this in two ways. First, they promote sectarianism by teaching or implying that their group is the only truly Christian group: No other groups can be trusted, and the only safety is found in this group under this leader's influence. The apostle John condemns Diotrophes for this in 3 John 1:9-10.

Second, they teach or imply that all major life decisions should be approved by them and the leadership structure over which they preside. Paul rebukes the Corinthians for submitting to this in 2 Corinthians 11:20.

7. *The successful Christian leader must show a track record (testimony) of grace over the use of money.*

Authentic Christian Leaders Teach and Model Financial Integrity

Fruitful Christian workers should normally be paid so they're able to live at a reasonable level (1 Tim. 5:17-18). However, they should be above reproach and free from the love of money (Titus 1:7), which includes living a modest lifestyle, generosity in personal financial giving, and the integrity to make spiritual decisions free from considerations of personal financial advantage. They will teach their flocks the importance of giving financially to God's work, but they will not use pressure tactics, and they will practice open accounting procedures.

8. *The successful Christian leader must be multi-skilled.*

Some modern church leaders fancy themselves businessmen, media figures, entertainers, psychologists, philosophers, or lawyers. Those notions contrast sharply with the way Scripture portrays spiritual leaders.

In II Timothy 2, for example, Paul uses seven different metaphors to describe the rigors of leadership. He pictures the minister as

- a teacher (v. 2)

- a soldier (v. 3)

- an athlete (v. 5)

- a farmer (v. 6)

- a workman (v. 15)

- a vessel (vv. 20-21)

- a slave (v. 24)

All those images evoke ideas of sacrifice, labor, service, and hardship. They speak eloquently of the complex and varied responsibilities of spiritual leadership. Not one of them makes leadership out to be glamorous. That's because it is not supposed to be glamorous.

Leadership in the church—and I'm speaking of every facet of spiritual leadership, not just the pastor's role—is not a mantle of status to be conferred on the church's aristocracy. It isn't earned by seniority, purchased with money, or inherited through family ties. It doesn't necessarily fall to those who are successful in business or finance. It isn't doled out on the basis of intelligence or talent. Its requirements are blameless character, spiritual maturity, and above all, a willingness to serve humbly.

Our Lord's favorite metaphor for spiritual leadership, a figure He often used to describe Himself, was that of a shepherd—one who tends God's flock. Every church leader is a shepherd. The word *pastor* itself means shepherd. It is appropriate imagery. A shepherd leads, feeds, nurtures, comforts, corrects, and protects. Those are responsibilities of every churchman. Shepherds are without status. In most cultures, shepherds occupy the lower rungs of society's ladder. That is fitting, for our Lord said, *"Let him who is the greatest among you become as the youngest, and the leader as the servant"* (Luke 22:26).

Under the plan God has ordained for the church, leadership is a position of humble, loving service. Church leadership is ministry, not management. Those whom God designates as leaders are called not to be governing monarchs but humble slaves; not slick celebrities but laboring servants. Those who would lead God's people must above all exemplify sacrifice, devotion, submission, and lowliness. Jesus Himself gave us the pattern when He stooped to wash His disciples' feet, a task that was customarily done by the lowest of slaves (John 13). If the Lord of the universe would do that, no church leader has a right to think of himself as a bigwig.

Shepherding animals is semi-skilled labor. There are no colleges which offer graduate degrees in shepherding. It isn't that difficult a job. Even a dog can be trained to guard a flock of sheep. In biblical times, young boys—David, for example—herded sheep while the older men did tasks that required more skill and maturity. Shepherding a spiritual flock is not so simple. It takes more than an unskilled laborer to be a spiritual shepherd. The standards are high, and the requirements, hard to satisfy (1 Tim. 3:17). Not everyone can meet the qualifications, and of those who do, few seem to excel at the task. Spiritual shepherding demands a godly, gifted, multi-skilled man of integrity. Yet he must maintain the humble perspective and demeanor of a boy shepherd.

With the tremendous responsibility of leading God's flock comes the potential for either great blessing or great judgment. Good leaders are doubly blessed (1 Tim. 5:17) and poor leaders are doubly chastened (v. 20), for *"from everyone who has been given much, much will be required"* (Luke 12:48). James 3:1 says, *"Let not many of you become teachers, my brethren, knowing that as such we will incur a stricter judgment."*

9. *The successful Christian leader should hold a position of responsibility in a local church.*

While the term "church member" never actually occurs in the New Testament, the concept is implicit. Christian believers clearly identified themselves with a local church, committed themselves to it, and became participating members and ministers in it. Barnabas and Saul did (Acts 11:26), and so did many other Christians (Romans 16).

How Does the Bible Define Church Membership?

The New Testament does not describe a local church full of attendees only, but rather describes a church of participating members and ministers. (See Romans 12:4-5, 1 Corinthians 12:12, and Ephesians 4:16). The moment we trust Jesus Christ as our Savior and Lord, we become members of the worldwide body of Christ, which is the church. This new position never changes and is eternal. However, to grow as a follower of Jesus, we must identify with and become a participating member in a specific local church wherever we live.

Church membership is not about signing a contract or joining a club. Yet what does membership offer? Membership gives a person a sense of identity (Ephesians 2:19-22). It provides a person with the opportunity to identify themselves as a true believer belonging to a local church. In becoming a formal member, a person is identifying themselves with similar beliefs, principles, and values. This provides a Christian believer with the foundation to express themselves as a child of God and as part of the body of Christ.

Luke tells us that these criteria "found approval with the entire congregation; and they chose Stephen, a man full of faith and of the Holy Spirit, and Philip, Prochorus, Nicanor, Timon, Parmenas and Nicolas" (Acts 6:5). So much for equal representation of Greek-speaking and Hebrew-speaking individuals! All seven of the men appointed had Greek names. And so by choosing seven from the Greek-speaking contingent, the apostles were ensuring that the Greek widows would no longer be shortchanged. With these seven men looking after the administrative tasks, the apostles were enabled to concentrate on the ministry of the Word and prayer. And what was the result? "The Word of God kept on spreading; and the number of the disciples continued to increase greatly in Jerusalem, and a great many of the priests were becoming obedient to the faith" (Acts 6:7).

10. *The successful Christian leader must have the following character traits:*

- Integrity
- Love
- Commitment to God
- Dependence on the Holy Spirit
- Compassion
- Vision

Character Crisis

Society has suffered terrible decay as the love of iniquity has trumped noble character. Sadly, what Western culture once regarded as virtuous and good has become almost unrecognizable. Take a few minutes to consider the importance of character, find its source, and commit yourself to the quest—the quest for character.

Character: It has an old-fashioned sound to it, like a faded relic of the Victorian era. We live in a materialistic culture where prestige, prosperity, and popularity are valued more than genuine integrity. In fact, personal character hardly seems to matter very much at all nowadays—at least in the realms of mass media, entertainment, politics, and pop culture. Only a few select moral qualities are still prized by society at large. They are chiefly liberal community values such as diversity, tolerance, and broad-mindedness. Sometimes they are even called virtues. But when traits like these are blended with hypocrisy or employed to justify some other iniquity, they become mere caricatures of authentic virtue.

Meanwhile, genuine individual virtue—the stuff of which true, timeless, praiseworthy character is made—has been formally relegated to the sphere of "personal" things best not talked about openly. These days, even an elected national leader's personal character is supposed to be treated as a wholly private matter.

As a result, our society's most prominent celebrities include countless people who are best known for gigantic character flaws. Notice, for example, the people who usually grace the covers of celebrity magazines. Very few are decent role models. Often they are people who exemplify the worst kinds of character traits. No morally sane, thinking parents would ever want for their own children to emulate the lifestyles or embrace the values of most of our society's best-known figures. Big personalities are highly revered anyway, because celebrity itself counts more than character in a society without any moral anchor. In fact, over the past few decades so many famous people have been charged with serious crimes that a cable television series is devoted exclusively to covering stories about their legal problems. Still, both the public and the media continue to confer celebrity status on more and more bizarre characters.

How have we come to this? The greatest cultures throughout human history have always reserved the highest positions of eminence and respect for true heroes—people who distinguish themselves by great self-sacrifice, moral excellence, or some truly great accomplishment. The only societies that confer celebrity status on immoral and villainous people have been cultures in serious decline and on the precipice of utter ruin.

One of the universally understood rules of thumb that governed Western society until a few short decades ago was that people who achieved fame had a duty to be wholesome role models. Even men and women who weren't really of sterling virtue in private sought to keep their character flaws hidden from the public—because if their moral defects became known, they lost their star status. Political figures could not remain in office if they were found culpable for any scandalous moral indiscretion. That is no longer the case. Today's celebrities proudly flaunt their decadence. With the rise of a massive entertainment industry in the second half of the twentieth century, celebrity became a cheap and shallow commodity. Honest character is now seen as totally optional—or worse, hopelessly unfashionable.

As a matter of fact, in certain segments of today's entertainment and music industries, authentic virtue would be practically incompatible with fame and success. Some of the best-known figures in the recording industry, for example, are avowed gangsters who openly glorify evil in their lyrics. It is frightening to contemplate the future of a society where so many people so lacking in character can attain celebrity status so easily—and often hang onto their fame and influence no matter what crimes they commit.

The Bible says that is exactly what happens when a society rejects God and thereby incurs His righteous judgment. Romans 1:21-32 describes the downward path of a culture abandoned to sin. Take note of the roster of evils that finally overwhelm every fallen society. The list closely resembles everything currently fashionable in the world of entertainment and celebrity:

"Even as they did not like to retain God in their knowledge, God gave them over to a debased mind, to do those things which are not fitting; being filled with all unrighteousness, sexual immorality, wickedness, covetousness, maliciousness; full of envy, murder, strife, deceit, evil-mindedness; they are whisperers, backbiters, haters of God, violent, proud, boasters, inventors of evil things, disobedient to parents, undiscerning, untrustworthy, unloving, unforgiving, unmerciful; who, knowing the righteous judgment of God, that those who practice such things are deserving of death, not only do the same but also approve of those who practice them" (Romans 1:28-32).

That describes our culture to the letter, doesn't it? People today literally entertain themselves with iniquity, heedlessly applauding those who sin most flagrantly. Society today makes celebrities of people who in our grandparents' generation would have been deemed the most contemptible rogues. Almost everything that used to be considered shameful is now celebrated. We therefore live in a culture where personal character and individual virtue are rapidly evaporating at almost every level. Virtue and infamy have traded places.

According to the Bible, God designed us to be men and women of exemplary character. He repeatedly commands us to pursue what is virtuous and shun what is evil. From cover to cover, in Scripture, iniquity is condemned and virtue is exalted. Clearly, we are supposed to be men and women of excellent character. We're commanded to *"hold fast what is good [and] abstain from every form of evil"* (1 Thessalonians 5:21-22).

But where do we go to learn how to do that? Popular culture will not point the way for us. Scripture alone is a reliable lamp for our feet and light for our path (Psalm 119:105). God's

Word points the way in the quest for character. The Bible contains numerous lists of positive character qualities. Second Peter 1:5-8, for example, gives a catalogue of virtues and urges us to add these to our faith. The fruit of the Spirit in Galatians 5, the qualities of authentic love in 1 Corinthians 13, and the Beatitudes in Matthew 5 all list similar traits that describe true excellence of character. Truly excellent character is actually a reflection of the moral nature of God Himself. For that reason, all virtues are interdependent and closely related. And all of them are the fruit of God's grace. As you study biblical virtue, may you perceive the true beauty of Christ's character and desire to see it reproduced in your own lives.

The Leader's Character

The Bible teaching about Christian leadership functions reveals that character and core values are crucial. Paul said those in Christian leadership are servants and stewards of the mysteries of God, and that *"it is required of stewards that one be found trustworthy"* (1 Corinthians 4:2).

In another place, Paul wrote, *"And the things which you have heard from me in the presence of many witnesses, these entrust to faithful men, who will be able to teach others also"* (2 Timothy 2:2; cf. 1 Thessalonians 2:5-6). The political detractors and accusers of Daniel concluded that *"they could find no ground of accusation or evidence of corruption, inasmuch as he was faithful, and no negligence or corruption was to be found in him"* (Daniel 6:4).

At the heart of the Christian leader must be integrity and honesty. The leader must be genuinely committed to the goals and values of the group they lead. The group also must recognize that quality in their leader. For Christian leadership then, the leader must be devoted to the values and purposes of Jesus Christ – and of the organization served. In fact, Christian leadership must be more than a role that is played. It must be a reality that is lived.

Management is doing things right; leadership is doing the right things."

Peter F. Drucker

Chapter 11

INTRODUCING THE REALITY OF HELL

He could not believe his eyes. This was the last place he had expected to be. No…no… this cannot be happening, he thought. This cannot be real; it's just a horrible nightmare, and I will soon wake up and find how untrue all of this is. He closed his eyes, took a deep breath, and waited just like his mother had taught him to do when he was a little boy.

"It is the best way to overcome your fears," she would say. "When you open your eyes you will find that none of these scary sights were really there after all. They will all go away."

He opened his eyes and realized that, for the first time since he had known his mother, she had been wrong. The shrieking, tormenting sounds of men and women screaming in pain was deafening; it was so horrible to watch as the flames consumed their bodies, and they tore at their flesh, ripping it apart, bleeding and still not getting the relief they sought. The smell of sulphur filled the air, and he felt himself choking. The worms that covered the men and women made looking at them a gruesome sight. This was worse than any horror movie he had ever seen. The difference was that this was not a movie, and the people were no actors; this was real, and he just could not take his eyes off it.

"I am not here and this is not happening," he said, and did not even realize he had spoken aloud until he heard another voice speak.

"Oh, yes, it is."

He turned, and before him stood the most handsome creature he had ever laid eyes on. He was beautiful and gracefully built. His hair fell about like a gleaming river of blackness, and his eyes shone like two black shining stones. Beauty and a coldness that could freeze the Atlantic radiated from the creature. The darkness within his heart showed clearly through his eyes.

"Who are you?" he asked the creature.

"One of the fallen angels," he replied casually, grinning broadly.

He moved away from him, and the demon, obviously amused by his reaction, said, "I guess you never thought you would end up here."

"Of course, I never expected that I would." He wanted to scream at this cohort of the devil. "I am too good to be in this dungeon!"

The fallen angel laughed. "Well, you had your chance…why didn't you make use of it? No…no…there is hardly time for regret, is there? You made your bed; it is time to lie on it. Your excuses won't work here."

His eyes turned even colder. "You had every opportunity to avoid ending up here but you decided to put it off. You did not expect death so soon did you? But it did come and so did judgment, and now you and I are here…together…where we belong." He smiled broadly. "Where are your earthly acquisitions now? Where are your beautiful wife and the expensive cars and homes? Let's not forget the many bank accounts. Where are they? None of those got you off, did they? Not even your wife's deep love for you could save you." He laughed again, but now it sounded more like a low growl. "Welcome to hell, sir."

The man stood there, transfixed, and his whole life passed before his eyes. He could not believe it was over. He could not bear the thought of going through such torture forever and ever and ever… Eternity!

"O God," he gasped. "God!"

He felt something touch him, and when he turned, he saw the demon still standing beside him, looking down at him as though he were dirt. "Are you going to just stand there?" he barked.

The man stared back at those horrible eyes afraid, not knowing what to do: and that was when the demon pushed him, and he fell into the abyss of fire. The fire licked at his flesh quickly, and thousands of worms crawled over his body, eating deeply into his flesh. He tore at his flesh, trying so hard to free himself from the torment. He screamed and screamed until his lungs felt sore; he cried until the tears in his eyes dried up. No one came to his rescue. No one tried to soothe his pain. No one would help him. He would never be free from this pain, this horror. He was thirsty and would have given anything at that moment for just a drop of water…[9]

---

9 This is just an imaginary description of what happens in hell.

"And as it is appointed unto men once to die, but after this the judgment" Heb 9:27 (KJV).

Hell is the place of eternal torments and pain, while heaven holds eternal bliss and glory. The greatest mistake any man can ever make is to end up in the abyss of fire called hell. Hell is not a feast hall with glittering lights, fancy table clothes, and a mouth-watering buffet. It is not the figment of some sadistic mind who is trying to stop the whole world from indulging in sinful acts. It is, in fact, a dreadful place created only for the devil and his rebels.

For a few moments, lie back and think of the billions of people currently in that abyss going through such torture and pain. Amongst these people are our fathers, mothers, uncles, aunts, sisters, brothers, children, nephews, and nieces. They languish, gnashing their teeth and wishing they had chosen to live right and accept the Word of Truth. Now, think of the teeming billions who are also on the journey toward this gruesome place at this very minute. I consider it a tragedy for anyone to trifle with sin. Its consequences are grave. Let us be concerned about the fact that all sinners will go to hell. Age, sex, educational background, social status, success, nationality or race will be irrelevant on the judgment day. God is no respecter of persons.

"But the fearful, and unbelieving, and the abominable, and murderers, and whoremongers, and sorcerers, and idolaters, and all liars, shall have their part in the lake which burneth with fire and brimstone: which is the second death." Rev 21:8 (KJV).

In hell, sinners shall drink the wrath of God like wine, and they shall be tormented with fire and brimstone.

"The same shall drink of the wine of the wrath of God, which is poured out without mixture into the cup of his indignation; and he shall be tormented with fire and brimstone in the presence of the holy angels, and in the presence of the Lamb: And the smoke of their torment ascendeth up for ever and ever: and they have no rest day nor night, who worship the beast and his image, and whosoever receiveth the mark of his name." Rev 14:10-11 (KJV).

"For, behold, the day cometh, that shall burn as an oven; and all the proud, yea, and all that do wickedly, shall be stubble: and the day that cometh shall burn them up, saith the LORD of hosts, that it shall leave them neither root nor branch." Mal 4:1 (KJV).

God dislikes sin, and if a Christian indulges in secret sins, the enemy will have an edge over him. If he dies in his sin, he will also end up in hellfire. For that reason, as Christians, we should be careful what we do. Accepting the Lord Jesus Christ is not enough. We should also be ready to work out our salvation with fear and trembling. Some Christians defend their sinful deeds by arguing that they are no longer in bondage; the Word of God is true, and as such, no one quarrels with their confession. Nevertheless, their actions and defenses should be critically examined in the light of God's commandments and righteous standards. Our liberties should not be used as an occasion for sinning. We have a responsibility to the billions of people who are daily walking toward the gates of hell. Our lifestyles, both in secret and in the open, could be their saving grace; we cannot afford to take our hands off the plough whenever it suits us. It is too deadly.

Ministers, do not compromise. Blood-guiltiness looms on the head of ministers who lead brethren astray. Our primary assignment is to preach the Word, in season and out. We should not bend the rules to please people. Like Jeremiah, we should speak the truth despite the persecutions we face. We should teach our flocks the weighty Bible doctrines concerning commitment, evangelism, holiness, heaven, and hell. We have more nominal Christians in our churches than born-again Christians. We have some members in our pews who are still dining with the devil. We should not take any of this lightly, but put our feet down and lead the people in the right path. Let us remember that in every passing minute, no less than a hundred people die, and the majority of them are trooping to hell.

The night is far spent; the day is gradually coming to an end. Let us wake up from our slumber and put aside slothfulness and hindrances that keep us from doing the work of our Father. Let us rescue the perishing and care for the dying. The time is now. The hymn writer says,

1. Rescue the perishing, care for the dying,
    Snatch them in pity from sin and the grave;
    Weep o'er the erring one, lift up the fallen,
    Tell them of Jesus, the mighty to save.

2. Though they are slighting Him, still He is waiting,
    Waiting the penitent child to receive;
    Plead with them earnestly, plead with them gently,
    He will forgive if they only believe.

3. Down in the human heart, crushed by the tempter,
    Feelings lie buried that grace can restore;
    Touched by a loving heart, wakened by kindness,
    Cords that are broken will vibrate once more.

4. Rescue the perishing, duty demands it
    Strength for your labor the Lord will provide;
    Back to the narrow way patiently win them,
    Tell the poor wand'rer a Savior has died.

Chorus:

Rescue the perishing, Care for the dying;

Jesus is merciful, Jesus will save.[10]

The devil, as a master of deceit, does everything he can to keep people from believing in the existence of a hell; but hell is a literal state of existence that will be the plight of all those who reject the Lord Jesus Christ.

TIM LAHAYE, Revelation Unveiled

---

[10] Fanny J. Crosby, 1820–1915
http://www.scriptureandmusic.com/Biographies/Crosby__Frances_Jane.pdf

Chapter 12

OUR HEAVENLY HOME

The classic architectural designs took our breath away. We could not help but stare and gape at these magnificent edifices that seemed to turn up everywhere we looked as we drove through Victoria Island toward the Lekki Peninsular area to see a friend of ours.

"Honey, that's a beautiful building…it's state-of-the-art," my wife said, pointing to yet another building.

"And so is that one," I replied, also pointing to another that had caught my eyes.

"It's all so glamorous, fantabulous, and supremely magnificent," Toyin uttered.

"Toyin, more of your lexicon, please," said Chris, an architect friend with whom we made the trip. We all laughed.

"These designs all have harmony, balance, rhythm, and dominance and the landscaping is indeed impressive. It's just so splendid." Toyin and I sat back, absorbed in Chris' professional description of the mansions.

"We have first-class designs all over the place, right here in Victoria Island and Ikoyi. Italian, German, Brazilian, and Hollywood archetypal, name them…they are all here," Chris said, and after a bit of a pause he added, "And so is the country's crude oil money which is in the hands of the privileged few who are leaders."

We sighed at the thought of how much money must have been spent on building these classics.

"If an earthly mansion is so magnificent, how beautiful heaven must be," Toyin wondered aloud.

I wondered, too; we became enraptured in the glory of that faraway city. Abraham and the old-time saints diligently sought that beautiful city, a city with which no city on earth could be compared. In heaven, there will be no poverty or societies overrun with materialism, crime, violence, and there will be no death. Its inhabitants will all have perfect bodies and minds. There will be no complaints of tooth decay, bad eyesight, or wrinkled skin. People will not suffer from cancer or migraines or AIDS. Everyone shall look like angels in their glorious bodies: ageless, healthy, and beautiful.

"And God shall wipe away all tears from their eyes; and there shall be no more death, neither sorrow, nor crying, neither shall there be any more pain: for the former things are passed away" Rev 21:4 (KJV).

The sweet and blessed fellowship between God and man will be fully enjoyed in heaven. Man and God will be forever united. Nothing can beat what awaits us in our heavenly home. Nothing can compare to the glory that is to come.

Some wonder at the reality of this place of eternal joy, peace, and life. Many cannot comprehend it. Some have come to the erroneous conclusions that heaven is just a channel through which our minds try to escape the pain and defeats we daily suffer in our earthly home. They feel that the deep search for universal peace, economic freedom, socio-political stability, perfect health for all, and everything good has birthed this desire which all that our world leaders and scientists have toiled from one generation to another to give us in this present world. Simply put, they wrongly conclude that heaven is not real. Poor and misguided people, we describe them. May the Father have mercy on them for they know not what they do or say. These are just deceptions of Satan, misleading and confusing people far from the truth so he can steal their eternity away from them.

Jesus puts this in perspective when he says;

"Ye are of your father the devil, and the lusts of your father ye will do. He was a murderer from the beginning, and abode not in the truth, because there is no truth in him. When he speaketh a lie, he speaketh of his own: for he is a liar, and the father of it." John 8:44 (KJV).

"The thief cometh not, but for to steal, and to kill, and to destroy: I am come that they might have life and that they might have it more abundantly" John 10:10 (KJV).

But the church knows better. We know what the Bible has said about heaven and to these things we hold. The world searches for global peace and a relief from suffering. World leaders convene frantically trying to find effective and permanent solutions to economic and perennial global socio-political problems. The UN and her agencies spend billions of dollars yearly to effect changes for progress. However, Jesus has made us understand that these searches, desires, and strategies will change nothing since everything that happens was premeditated by God. These are signs which tell the enlightened Church of Christ—who can read the writings on the wall—to prayerfully and laboriously prepare for the Lord's coming.

The rapture is the first phase of the Second Coming of Christ. All living saints will be translated, and all those who died in Christ will be resurrected and meet the Lord Jesus in the skies. In the second phase of His coming, those who will escape the great tribulation will partake in the marriage supper of the Lamb where they will be rewarded for all their deeds while they were on earth. Heaven is therefore not a dream, but a hope that is true and sure.

Jesus said emphatically:

"In my Father's house are many mansions: if it were not so, I would have told you. I go to prepare a place for you." John 14:2 (KJV).

Stephen was a man full of faith and of the Holy Ghost. He did great wonders and miracles amongst the people of God. He was martyred for his vibrant faith, and before he died he saw heaven open:

"When they heard these things, they were cut to the heart, and they gnashed on him with their teeth. But he, being full of the Holy Ghost, looked up steadfastly into heaven, and saw the glory of God, and Jesus standing on the right hand of God, And said, 'Behold, I see the heavens opened, and the Son of man standing on the right hand of God.'" Acts 7:54-56 (KJV).

More Visions of Heaven

For generations, other believers have recounted their visions of heaven. God has shown them this heavenly home and they testify of it.

Buddy Harris...

Buddy was a former Virginia state trooper, who was smashed between two cars and proclaimed dead. A motorist who was driving at a speed of 65 mph under the influence of marijuana and alcohol caused the accident. Buddy, however, came back to life, and he also shares his experience:

"Regaining consciousness, I stumbled around the side of their car. Then I crawled into their back seat. Blood poured from my body. "Get out of my car!" the woman screamed. "You're bleeding all over my carpet!"

Despite being weak and groggy, I obeyed. Slowly getting out, I wandered about twenty steps before I collapsed. Soon after, the rescue squad car arrived. In vain, they tried to get a heartbeat or a faint pulse. After thirty minutes of trying to find vital signs, the emergency workers pulled the sheet over my face. The time was 10:23 p.m. I was proclaimed dead. They turned their attention from my lifeless body to cleaning up the accident scene. With my body headed for the Richmond morgue, they were not in a big rush.

For me, everything went pitch black. After I passed out on the highway that night, I found myself before the darkest hole I have ever seen. I felt like I was trapped in a deep hole, yet I felt no pain or fear. Emerging from this charcoal air were thousands upon thousands of hands from the wrist down. They came at me like waves grabbing at my body but not touching me. I have been asked what this was, before I ever discussed this publicly in giving my testimony. I asked God to help me not to mislead anyone in explaining it. For what I endured, I believe was the valley of the shadow of death. As the twenty-third Psalm says, *"Yea though I walk through the valley of the shadow of death, I shall fear no evil for thou art with me."*

"One day you, too, will walk through that valley if you are a Christian. Satan will grab all he wants. I believe that is what he was trying to do that night, along with his angels; vainly trying to make one last snatch at God's child. Those hands fluttered at me for what seemed like two or three minutes; then I found myself bathed in a very bright light --the whitest, brightest light I have ever seen. When I looked around, it was just as white above me as it was in the distance.

Have you ever had one of those times when you felt like you could reach up and touch a piece of heaven? Even felt like you are going to burst wide open and just did not know what you would do? Multiply that a thousand fold, and you may have some idea of the unspeakable joy I felt as I stood there. Glory, happiness, and peace filled my soul. I know why we will need a new body when we get to heaven: Our earthly ones will not be able to contain the radiance. Ahead in the distance, I saw a large door. It looked like a thousand rainbows were pouring out of that door. It was the most beautiful sight I had ever seen, the most dazzling colors (and with four children and fifty boxes of crayons around the house, I know my colors). Attracted by the sight, I began walking towards it.

As I drew closer, I felt like the joy would cause my body to split in two. I felt inadequate trying to paint a picture of this scene. God says in his words that we have not seen or heard the things he has prepared for us. That's true. Had I made it to the door, I believe my loved ones would have already read and mourned my passing. Meanwhile, I would be dancing on the hills of glory, wrapping my hands around Moses and Abraham, and rejoicing in His presence. However, when I got six feet from the door, I woke up.

It's been more than twelve years since this happened, and for a long time, I was petrified to tell anyone about it. For some reason, God brought me back to life twenty-three minutes after the paramedics pronounced me dead at the scene. When I woke up, they were wheeling me down the hallway towards the morgue's cold storage area.

"A trooper named Sonny Dobbins, who has since died, was clutching the cart. Sonny was a mountain of a man. I have never seen him cry before. He was now. As I was trying to yank the sheet off my face, I saw the lights of the hallway. Blood had matted itself to my face so it was hard to remove. When I finally got the sheets off, I had no idea what had transpired. Looking at the fellow trooper, I asked, "Sonny, what happened?"

He could only stammer with amazement, "Ahh! But you are supposed to be dead!"

They whisked me to the hospital. I was hospitalized and spent three months recuperating at home. I also had two hundred thousand dollars' worth of plastic surgery done to my face. It did not really change much: I still have a big nose and baggy eyes. But they closed my facial wounds so there would not be scars.

Remember I said I was out for twenty-three minutes? After four minutes you are supposed to have brain damage. While I was in the hospital, doctors told my wife, "We don't know if he'll ever walk again." The bottom line is I'm still healthy, running, and working out."[11]

Roberts Liardon in his book *I Saw Heaven* relates:

"The first thing I saw in heaven was the golden streets with golden curbs. The curbs are lined with flowers in all colors of the rainbow. I looked down and made a mad dash for the grass. Jesus turned to say something to me, but I was gone. I was standing on the grass with my eyes and mouth wide open in surprise.

Jesus asked, "What are you doing over there?"

I replied with these two words "Golden streets." Some parts of the street looked like our gold on earth while other parts were as clear as crystal. I could see through them.

Jesus laughed and laughed. He laughed so hard I thought he would never stop. He said "Come here."

I said "No, these streets are gold. I cannot walk on them. The only time I have seen gold was in the form of a ring on a person's hand. I cannot walk on these streets."

But Jesus beckoned, "Come on." He laughed harder. As he walked over to me to get me back on the street, he said "These streets are made for my brothers and sisters. You are my brother, so enjoy them."[12]

These testimonies all tell of the splendid and unparalleled glory of heaven, which the apostle John described two thousand years ago in the book of Revelation. The occultist, the astrologist, the adherents of Eastern religions, the ECKist, the freemasons, the AMORC member, and other apostate heretics make one want to weep bitterly. Most of their beliefs and teachings on hell and heaven contain incredible heresies. Some of them practice astral

---

[11] The Story of Buddy Harris about Heaven

[12] Roberts Liardon, *I saw Heaven*, Bethany House Pub (June 1987)

projections, an out-of-body experience that enables the soul and spirit to project out of the physical body and roam freely to whatever dimension in the spiritual world it desires.

The so-called grandmasters, who have unfortunately misled millions all over the world, consider heaven and hell as mere planes and dimensions that can be reached at will. The devil, that grand deceiver and killer, is making mincemeat of many of these people, and they, in turn, are allowing him to have his way. Eternity is too transcendent for finite man's manipulations. We, who know the truth, should therefore hold fast to our eternity as the day approaches. Let us draw near to the Lord who is our comfort, guide, protector, encourager, and strength. We are on a pilgrimage here on earth. We should not feel relaxed, for this is not our place of rest. Let us fight to enter through the narrow gate.

"Enter ye in at the strait gate: for wide is the gate, and broad is the way, that leadeth to destruction, and many there be which go in there at: Because strait is the gate, and narrow is the way, which leadeth unto life, and few there be that find it." Matt 7:13-14 (KJV).

Yes, the cost of going through the narrow way is enormous, but the rewards are handsome and fulfilling. Therefore, brethren, heaven in focus should be the sun and energy of the believer's spiritual life. The glory we will enjoy eventually is worth every suffering we encounter on this earth.

"But as it is written, Eye hath not seen, nor ear heard, neither have entered into the heart of man, the things which God hath prepared for them that love him." 1 Cor 2:9 (KJV)

Heaven is not here, it's There. If we were given all we wanted here,

our hearts would settle for this world rather than the next.

God is forever luring us up and away from this one,

wooing us to Himself and His still invisible Kingdom,

where we will certainly find what we so keenly long for.

Author: Elisabeth Elliot in **Keep a Quiet Heart** .

Chapter 13

MANAGING TIME EFFECTIVELY

The way we spend each instant of life should actually determine the success, happiness, or failures we get out of it. The Now time is the only available moment we have to develop our latent resources and attend to our families, career, recreation, and kingdom business. The profits we can make from this valuable asset which God has equally given to each and every one of us are enormous.

So many Christians go through life lamenting that they do not have enough time to serve God and faithfully fulfill their ministries. The problem is not really that there is no time; the problem has more to do with time management. For one to be successful in all his endeavors including his spiritual and kingdom life, he has to be intensely determined and efficient at time usage. He has to have a time planned out for all his activities. We have Christians who hardly keep time. They always arrive late to every appointment. They totally forget that time waits for no man, and yet they find it convenient to claim God's promises and expect Him to fulfill all of them in their lives at the appointed time. God is conscious of time. He watches over His word to perform it at the fullness of time. Hence, our attitude should change.

Solomon was indeed correct when he said:

"To everything there is a season, and a time to every purpose under the heaven:

A time to be born and a time to die;

A time to plant, and a time to pluck up that which is planted;

A time to kill and a time to heal;

A time to break down and a time to build up;

A time to weep, and a time to laugh;

A time to mourn and a time to dance;

A time to cast away stones and a time to gather stones together;

A time to embrace, and a time to refrain from embracing;

A time to get, and a time to lose;

A time to keep, and a time to cast away" Eccl 3:1-7 (KJV).

The question now is how we can efficiently manage our time. How can we put all our activities together and do each and every one of them? Time management helps put the life of any individual in balance. The men and women we call successful in our world today are good time managers. They do not waste time. Like the sons of Issachar, they understand the times, and know exactly what to do. They make every second, minute, hour, and day count.

Be in Charge of Your Time

Avoid laziness

The first thing you need to learn is that laziness—indulging in activities that will not profit your mind, spirit, or body—only moves you closer to disappointment, sickness, failure, and poverty. Anyone and anything that will cause you to lose opportunities is your enemy. If you find out that you spend more hours watching television than you spend doing productive things like studying for an exam or reading your Bible, then you need to put the television back in its box.

Watch who your friends are

The kind of people you hang out with will also determine how efficiently you use your time. You need to break up relationships with so-called friends who spend time talking about others and hardly talk about things that could benefit you. You are not a garbage can. You are a potential success. Find people who are goal-oriented and spend time with them. Hang out with people who want to impact their world men and women who do not only sit back and dream but take positive steps to actualizing their dreams. Make these people your friends.

Have goals and plan your time wisely to accomplish them

The next thing to do is plan. What do you want to accomplish? What are your goals and aspirations? A plan helps you define your purpose and activities. By working with a plan, you can set your performance standard and know if you are making progress or not. Your clearly defined objective keeps everything thoroughly organized and makes life less clumsy for you.

We have two plan ranges to consider planning. First, there is the long-range plan. This is the plan that details what you can accomplish in a long period of time. A short-range plan breaks these long-range plans into smaller bits. It makes them attainable and doable. Short-range plans bring you closer to your goals. They take the burden off trying to accomplish it all in one day and help you to make daily moves and daily progress. They are, in fact, only small parts of the bigger picture which is your long range plan.

In Genesis 1, God had a goal. He wanted to create man solely for His pleasure. Man was God's long-range plan. He sat down to consider what man would need and how to make sure he would be most comfortable.

Then He began to put everything in place. He did not create everything at once, even though we know He has power enough to have done that. He chose to prioritize. He created the world in an order, according to their level of importance. So, as you can see, planning is, in fact, an idea that is as old as the world itself, and not some new technique borrowed from one of those "how to do it in order to make it" books that fill our bookstores.

Now we move on to the next stage. Ask yourself what you want to accomplish each day, and write the tasks down according to their importance. Allocate appropriate time for each item in order to have a deadline. That will keep you focused. Call your daily list your "to do" list and keep it close to you, in a place where you are likely to find it so you can be reminded.

Be committed to your goals

The hardest part of accomplishing any goal is doing it. Commitment is what will take the concepts out of your mind and create the business you dream. It is what will make your spouse and children love you for the rest of your life. Simply put, commitment is what will make your dreams come true. Anything worth getting in life comes with a price, and that also includes your heavenly home. That means that, although you really would like to sit back and laze around for a few minutes, leaving the things on your "to do" list undone, you do not have to fall to that temptation. Working in an ordered way is the one thing most human beings find so hard to do, but remember that paying the price also means being disciplined. This is what will put your name in the roll call of the successful.

Avoid procrastination like a plague

Procrastination has no advantages. It kills dreams and will never make great men. It leaves no food on the table, no money in our pocket, and, of course, puts no stars in our crowns in heaven. For you to bring your desires to pass, break that hindrance called procrastination. Procrastination never gets the job done.

Avoid time wasters

There are those of us who understand these principles and apply them, but who have made little or no results from doing so. There are certain time wasters that keep us from realizing our desired objectives. These time wasters not only deprive those in the secular world from making progress, but they also affect ministers, church administrators, and departmental leaders. At the end of the day, they all feel burnt out and stressed. These time wasters have been outlined below with ways by which they can be overcome. This will help us all to efficiently manage time and increase our performance standard.

Impatience: Success is not an overnight phenomenon. You do not go to bed poor and wake up in the morning with a sack of gold by your side. What we all call success is just many days, weeks, months, and years of toiling and failing and restarts and more toiling and even more failing and restarts and jumping over hurdles and finding lasting solutions to problems.

No child walks the day he is born. No seed grows the day it is planted. So know that even with your priorities outlined, you might not have the results you so desire immediately. You need patience and persistence. Impatience will only steal away from you what could have been yours but did not get in your hand because you were in too much of a hurry. If something does not work as it should, then don't stop there: keep working on it until it does. That principle keeps the dream alive.

Being passive and not affirmative: Passivity is a time waster. It makes you a dumping ground for things you ought not to do, but do anyway because you are afraid to say no to someone.

Fear God, not people: You need not be afraid of people if you trust God. He has not given unto us the spirit of fear but of boldness. We can stand and talk and get what we wish even when it is not convenient for us. The three Hebrew children stood before Nebuchadnezzar and fearlessly told him that they would not bow to his golden image. Jesus was not afraid of the Pharisees or Sadducees. He faced them and spoke the truth and the whole world respected Him for it.

Carrying undue "loads" from others: Your "to do" list is the detailed formulation of your program. Adding someone else's burden, especially when you know it can be avoided, keeps you at a loss. Learn to say "no" politely to favors and jobs that stand in the way of accomplishing your goals.

Set your priorities, learn to delegate: Having too many things to do at the same time is dangerous. Establishing your priorities makes life easier to navigate. But most of us do not know what should be on our list and what should be delegated to others. Some of us in leadership positions do not know how to delegate duties to our subordinates; we do not trust their judgments and have no confidence in them. So we take on their jobs as well as our own and end up stressed, unable to do all we set out to do in the first place.

We need to know our limits. If you are a departmental leader in your church or organization, train your subordinates to do what you are doing. That leaves you more room to get other things done. Let them make mistakes and then correct them. Eliminate mistrust; teach them to organize the meeting, record minutes accurately, make decisions, and follow them up. Delegate duties to all members of your team and give them deadlines. **Then leave them to do it and focus on your own list.**

Set a deadline for whatever you set out to do: Not having deadlines is a vague way to live and prevents you from accomplishing great things. Put time range to your goals. How long do you want to spend in accomplishing these goals? Note the timeframe; this will help keep you focused, serious, and hardworking. Let us all cultivate a sense of the value of time. Apostle Paul admonishes us rightly, saying; *"See then that ye walk circumspectly, not as fools, but as wise, redeeming the time, because the days are evil."* Eph 5:15-16 (KJV). And in Colossians 4:5, Paul further says; *"Walk in wisdom toward them that are without, redeeming the time"*

We should never forget that we will account for every second, minute, and hour we have been given when we finally stand before the Lord. See every passing day as another opportunity given to you by the Holy Spirit to produce in every aspect of your life. Stop making excuses for why you are not witnessing or fasting, praying or studying the Word. Instead, start making amends, start strategizing, for time waits for no man. Man makes out time for everything; do not misuse this valuable asset. Use it wisely. Begin now.

God hath given to man a short time here upon earth;
and yet upon this short time, eternity depends.-- Jeremy Taylor

Chapter 14

MY DARLING JESUS

Jesus' performed outstanding miracles and wonders. He raised the dead, cleansed the lepers, and exercised authority over the forces of darkness. He changed man's destiny in a profound manner. He was sought by the needy, the sick, the oppressed, the tormented, and seekers of the divine light. He gave Himself totally and completely to man throughout His lifetime.

However, the religious authorities of that time—the Sanhedrin, the Pharisees, and the Sadducees—became greatly alarmed at His popularity and successes. Every word He spoke was accepted by the teeming thousands of people that heard Him except some of these religious people. The miracles He performed further increased their faith and belief in Him. Jesus did not desist from speaking the truth and He spoke with confidence. Some of the truth exposed the wrongdoings and hypocrisy of the religious authorities, and they became hostile opposers. They could not stand to be humiliated, and their dislike for Him created a deep hatred in their hearts. They found His personality so puzzling. There was something totally extraordinary about Him. He had been born in a manger to by a virgin after an angel made the announcement to His mother;

"And the angel said unto her, Fear not, Mary: for thou hast found favor with God. And, behold, thou shalt conceive in thy womb, and bring forth a son, and shalt call his name JESUS. He shall be great, and shall be called the Son of the Highest: and the Lord God shall give unto him the throne of his father David: And he shall reign over the house of Jacob forever; and of his kingdom there shall be no end. Then said Mary unto the angel, how shall this be, seeing I know not a man? And the angel answered and said unto her, The Holy Ghost

shall come upon thee, and the power of the Highest shall overshadow thee: therefore also that holy thing which shall be born of thee shall be called the Son of God." Luke 1:30-35 (KJV).

In the small village of Nazareth, amongst the cattle and horses, this great King was born. Shepherds arrived at the scene to worship Him and wise men came from far countries to give Him gifts. Now Then He revealed things the whole world had never known: He had come to earth just to die.

He was betrayed by one He loved and cherished. The nails were placed upon His hands and hammered until they pierced through them, nailing them to the cross. The spikes joined His feet. The crown of thorns placed on His head pierced through His flesh and blood gushed out of the wounds upon His face. His back was torn by the lashes of the whips the soldiers had flogged Him with. He was stripped naked of every single garment, fully displayed to complete his humiliation. He hung on the cross like a common criminal. He was afflicted, oppressed, and mocked by the embittered crowds. Their taunting and relishing of his public disgrace knew no bounds.

Yet, in that darkness, even with so much persecution, rejection, and torture, His voice cried out loud and clear, *"Father, forgive them for they know not what they do."* Before He drew His last breath, He cried out for all in heaven, on earth, and underneath the earth to hear *"It is finished."* And indeed it was finished. Jesus' decision to die on the cross for me had saved me from the clutches of hell forever.

"And, having made peace through the blood of his cross, by him to reconcile all things unto himself; by him, I say, whether they be things in earth, or things in heaven. And you, that were sometime alienated and enemies in your mind by wicked works, yet now hath he reconciled in the body of his flesh through death, to present you holy and unblameable and unreproveable in his sight." Col 1:20-22 (KJV).

What would my life be like had He not given His life for me? Perhaps I would be addicted to drugs, or who knows…maybe I would be by now, languishing in hell. I thank my darling Lord for going through all that pain and torture for me. He opened for me wellsprings of joy and everlasting life. He liberated me from sin and death and made me an heir with Him.

I made up my mind since the day I gave my life to Christ to live each day proclaiming His goodness to all mankind. My enlistment in His army means only one thing: I am now an enemy of hell. The devil knows I will not prattle and play frivolities with his wicked kingdom. I will run the race I have been given and use every single ounce of strength within me to make sure others also hear of the goodness of the Lord and of His saving grace. The whole church must take the gospel of our darling Lord to the whole world. Every believer is a minister. You do not need to be ordained. Christ is saying to us:

"Ye are the light of the world. A city that is set on a hill cannot be hid. Neither do men light a candle and put it under a bushel, but on a candlestick; and it giveth light unto all that are in

the house. Let your light so shine before men, that they may see your good works, and glorify your Father which is in heaven." Matt 5:14-16 (KJV).

Let us therefore abolish that which is evil and cleave to what is good. Let us obey His commandment and live blameless lives unto His glorious appearing. We should not be slothful in business but fervent in the Spirit, serving our Lord. We should also note that we cannot indulge in secret sins and fight this battle with the devil. We have to choose a side to be on. At the great judgment day, all shall be revealed, including pretenses and sinful habits.

"Neither is there any creature that is not manifest in his sight: but all things are naked and opened unto the eyes of him with whom we have to do." Heb 4:13 (KJV).

What we do in the secret place is open before the Lord. He sees our thoughts. We cannot hide our deeds from Him. Psalm 139 also tells us this. As believers, we must shine brighter than the sun in this perverse and crooked world. We must be modest even when ostentation and immodesty are in vogue. Our lives should draw sinful men to Christ, not make them turn away. Jesus has given so much for us and we in turn should give so that others can have what we have been given. We should daily make Him proud of us.

The winds of healing, deliverance, power, and great revival and wonders are blowing all over the world. From South Korea to Nigeria, many souls bound by the devil have been set free. In India, there has been the destruction of communism and that country is having a good taste of the Good News. The Asian and Latin American countries are also witnessing a tremendous outpouring of the Holy Ghost. Where economic progress and world leaders have failed, Jesus is reigning like the mighty KING HE IS.

Life indeed is a must journey every human must experience. It is like a jig -saw puzzle that must be fitted together to form a complete picture of whom God intends you to be. It might take some time, but God who is ever faithful, would complete the picture at the appointed time.

Bro Dewumi, as I fondly call the author, has clearly drawn a picture of true life experiences that is set to impact and rightly counsel the readers on life issues so as to take the right decisions.The author rounded off the discuss with the greatest decision any human must take to sustain an eternal relationship with his or her maker.It is the decision to accept the gift of eternal relationship through Jesus Christ. This book is recommend to everyone who desires live a victorious life and sustain a true relationship.

Titi Adeaga

ABOUT THE BOOK

Every event of our life counts—now and in eternity. God uses all that happens to us to bring glory to his name; but we should yield ourselves to him. Our life or walk of faith has a standard established by God. When we graciously follow this standard pattern designed by God we have a meaningful life—spiritually, physically, socially, psychologically and career-wise. *Made for Relationship* is a story and testimony to this truth. In *Made for Relationship*, Dr. Alabi shows us,

- How the grace and divine hand of God can lead us to have victory over sins and situations that can wreck our faith, life, marriage and professional career.

- The testimonies, the experiences, and the insights into how the basic issues of Christian life can impact our professional practice in market.

- The possibility of having relationships with colleagues and friends [even the opposite sex] without indulging in illicit sexual and immoral acts.

- How the grace of God, and our determination to fear and please God in all areas of our life, can bring a blissful, peaceful, and successful existence, even when value and virtues are fading away in our contemporary humanistic world.

The book shows and teaches that Christians can live, work, and practice their faith in the market place and shine for the Lord. It is not a fiction but a narration from true live events and experiences over some years. We need to learn from this testimony.

"God's plan is to make much of the man, far more of him than of anything else. Men are God's method. The Church is looking for better methods; God is looking for better men. "
— E.M. Bounds, Power Through Prayer

CPSIA information can be obtained
at www.ICGtesting.com
Printed in the USA
BVHW010155201218
536066BV00009B/491/P

9 781545 606209